Bioinspiration in Business and Management

Bioinspiration in Business and Management

Innovating for Sustainability

Taryn Mead, PhD

 BUSINESS EXPERT PRESS

Bioinspiration in Business and Management: Innovating for Sustainability

First published in 2018 by
Business Expert Press, LLC
222 East 46th Street, New York, NY 10017
www.businessexpertpress.com

ISBN-13: 978-1-63157-224-1 (paperback)
ISBN-13: 978-1-63157-225-8 (e-book)

Business Expert Press Principles for Responsible Management Education Collection

Collection ISSN: 2331-0014 (print)
Collection ISSN: 2331-0022 (electronic)

Cover and interior design by Exeter Premedia Services Private Ltd., Chennai, India

First edition: 2018

10 9 8 7 6 5 4 3 2 1

Printed in the United States of America.

Abstract

Many organizations have found themselves well advanced in their sustainability strategies and reaching the limits of progress made through eco-efficiency measures and regulatory compliance. Looking for novel approaches and solutions, many managers are turning to bioinspiration and related fields such as biomimicry, nature-inspired innovation, circular economy, and cradle to cradle as tools for sustainability-oriented innovation. This innovation paradigm has been gaining popularity across disciplines in recent decades as the world grapples with the challenge of sustainable development. This book offers a succinct guide and overview for managers and sustainability professionals who are interested in exploring various aspects of business inspired by nature. With applicability ranging from technological, organizational, and system-building innovations, there is a broad realm of possibilities that suit a manager's scope of influence regardless of their position within the organization. This book aims to exhibit the applications of business inspired by nature that extend beyond the boundaries of the organization and encourage open innovation with novel partners in unlikely scenarios, with all partners aligned by the principles of natural systems.

Keywords

biomimicry, bioinspired, bioinspiration, biomimetics, circular economy, cradle to cradle, corporate sustainability, eco-innovation, green innovation, human-nature relationship, industrial ecology, learning from nature, nature inspired, sustainability, sustainable innovation, sustainability-oriented innovation

Contents

CHAPTER 1

Introduction

Bio-What?

As a bioinspired innovation consultant and academic, I have had many conversations that go something like this:

New friend: "So what do you do for work?"

Me: "I work in a discipline called biomimicry—bios-, meaning 'life' and—mimesis, meaning 'to imitate.'"

New friend: [Puzzled, yet intrigued expression.]

Me: "The premise is that all of the organisms living on the planet know how to be sustainable, and there's a lot that humans can learn from these other organisms. I help architects, engineers, designers and business people learn from nature for more sustainable solutions to their challenges."

New friend: "Wow, how interesting. Can you give me an example?"

This is where it gets trickier to explain. There are innumerable examples of bioinspiration, dating back to early human civilizations. Leonardo Da Vinci was a well-known practitioner of biomimetic innovation. Modern-day examples usually involve shiny gadgets, high-tech developments, and complex systems—alternatives to existing chemicals and materials, and complex supply chain infrastructures that hardly resemble living systems without carefully articulated metaphors. The diversity of possible examples makes the perspective of the audience an important detail when choosing which story of a biomimetic innovation will be most compelling for the listener. The applications of bioinspiration are as diverse as the users, ranging from product design to architecture to engineering to social applications.

For the purposes of this book, I will be addressing you, the reader, as a busy business professional who wants to know the basics of bioinspiration and all its various manifestations. We will focus on those applications that are most relevant to the management professional, though sector-specific examples will also be presented for the purposes of explanation. Given that this area of research and innovation has been growing at exponential rates in recent decades (Bonser 2006), it is imperative that managers become familiar with the various terms, perspectives, tools, and approaches to apply nature-inspired innovation to enterprise sustainability.

My goal both as an academic and a consultant is to enable practitioners to reconnect with natural systems in such a way that they feel empowered to bring sustainability lessons from nature to the lab, the design table, and the boardroom. Bioinspiration purists may scoff at my inclusive approach to nature-inspired innovation and decry that what I am referring to is actually several different fields of study. But as an academic myself, I find many of the differentiations between terms to be the splitting of hairs that is not necessarily helpful to advance the cause of learning from nature in practical settings.

In my research with multinationals using bioinspired innovation strategies, their internal narratives varied quite substantially. For some organizations, bioinspired terms such as biomimicry, cradle-to-cradle, industrial ecology, and circular economy represent discrete projects with their own lifespans, budgets, and outcomes. For other organizations, these innovation methods are used interchangeably and are viewed more broadly under a company narrative of *learning from nature* for sustainability.

For this reason, I will approach a broad range of topics under the more inclusive umbrella of bioinspiration or bioinspired innovation to include approaches such as biomimicry, cradle-to-cradle, industrial ecology, and circular economy. Given the amount of overlap in these areas of focus, it seems appropriate to provide conceptual distinctions as an FYI for the reader, but generally more helpful to present the practical applications that make these approaches appropriate for various levels of sustainability-oriented innovation.

If you are like the thousands of people interested in bioinspiration that I have encountered in my career, your interest is likely motivated by one of three curiosities: sustainability, nature-nerding, or innovation. For those of you driven primarily by sustainability, you likely have an interest in or workplace need for sustainability, and you are always looking for new tools for your sustainability toolkit. For those of you who self-identify as nature nerds or closet biologists, you likely have a deep connection with living systems already and you are seeking ways to deepen that connection. If you are primarily interested in innovation, you see biological strategies as a vast pool of innovative fodder for new products, services, and strategies. It is likely that all three of these aspects apply to you to some degree. Over the years, most of my students have demonstrated a combination with greater or lesser emphasis on one of the three. It may be helpful to take a moment to identify whether any of these entry points is more important for you.

Why are You Interested in Bioinspiration?
- **Sustainability Gurus** "Sustainability is a major aspect of my career and bioinspiration is a great addition to my toolkit."
- **Nature Nerds** "I've always loved nature and am excited to learn more about incorporating these values into my work."
- **Innovation Seekers** "Innovation and creative problem solving is my passion and nature offers millions of novel innovative solutions."

While this book will address each of the three, there are many other resources available that emphasize bioinspiration at the interface of each aspect. For our purposes, these topics will be woven throughout the text in various ways, but perhaps keep a reflective eye on where you stand as well, as a means to guide your introduction to bioinspired innovation. Three different types of biomimetic innovations are found in corporate settings, broadly categorized as technological, organizational, and systems-building innovations.

Descriptions of Types of Bioinspired Innovations
- **Technological innovations** include product, process, material, and manufacturing changes that are inspired by biological models.
- **Organizational innovations** include changes to management strategies (e.g., applying swarm theory to team dynamics), trainings on bioinspiration, or other activities that encourage

employees to learn from biological models to solve their
workplace challenges.
- **Systems-building innovations** are those that intentionally
extend beyond the boundaries of the organization to
create changes to systems of production and consumption,
socioecological systems, and socioeconomic systems.

Figure 1.1 demonstrates how these three categories can be viewed in
a nested relationship with technologies embedded in organizations, and
organizations embedded in larger systems.

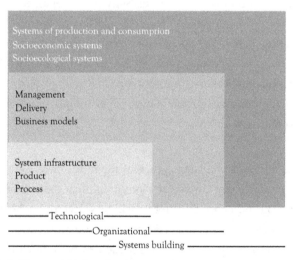

Figure 1.1 Types of bioinspired innovations

Source: Mead (2017).

These three categories will be mentioned in the later sections of the
book, but the main objective of making these distinctions here is to shed
any preconceived notions about what bioinspiration might mean to the
reader before beginning this book. While much of the popular media
on bioinspiration has focused on product and material design, there is a
tremendous amount of work underway in which biological strategies are
influencing various layers of corporate innovation. The following chapters
will pull apart these layers into a practical conceptual framework that
emphasizes the role of the manager in the application of bioinspiration.

Why Bioinspiration Now?

Does it seem like you are hearing a lot more about bioinspiration lately? It is likely that you actually are. From 1985 until 2005, the number of patents related to bioinspired innovation increased faster than the overall rate of all published patents (Bonser 2006), and there is even an economic index tracking the progress of biomimetic innovation in the economy (The Fermanian Business and Economic Institute 2010). At the time of writing, there is currently a process underway to develop ISO standards related to biomimetics. International NGOs have been turning to bioinspiration as a source of new inspiration, including the Worldwatch Institute and the International Union for Conservation of Nature.

To zoom out at a larger level of historical and social perspective, several authors have posed that we are in the midst of a paradigm shift from a mechanistic or anthropocentric worldview to an ecocentric worldview that is guiding much of our thinking today (e.g., Capra and Luisi 2014; Du Plessis and Brandon 2014; Dubberly 2012; Hutchins 2012). The overall argument goes something like this: For most of human history (and still today in more traditional societies), much of human interaction with the earth has been grounded in the perception of a living planet and an ecocentric worldview. This carried the advancement of human societies through tens of thousands of years of our existence. However, since the 16th century, the rise of capitalism, the Industrial Revolution, and the spread of Christianity frequently suppressed ecocentric views as anti-progress, evil, and dangerous to a modernizing society. Think *burning witches*. A few key concepts emerged during this era that have guided much of Western development and further shunned an ecocentric worldview.

The first is the notion that living things could be viewed as analogous to mechanistic systems and interactions. Francis Bacon, largely credited with developing the scientific method, had a knack for understanding things in terms of parts rather than wholes. Much of modern science is based on the premise that breaking down complexity into manageable units will enable a complete understanding of a complex phenomenon. And indeed, this has given us enormous gains in science, medicine, and technology. However, in the process, we have lost some of our ability to sense, interpret, and respond to systemic changes because much of our educational process is designed to help us understand constituent parts in a mechanistic way, rather than a systemic way. This is the essence of a mechanistic worldview.

The second notion that has profoundly shaped the Western worldview, chronologically paralleling the first notion, is the biblical mandate that humans shall have dominion over the earth. While there are many modern interpretations of this *Dominion Clause*, as I will call it, most interpretations put humans on top of all food chains and in charge of all ecosystems, with the primary responsibility of *subduing* nature for human use along the way. With the rise of this perspective, humans are not interdependent and interconnected with ecological systems as previous cultures had maintained for tens of thousands of years. Wilderness became something *out there*, and it was a very scary place that needed taming. This gave rise to an anthropocentric worldview that dominates the human development narrative today.

So, let us arrive back at the present to assess where we are today. We have come a long way in the last 500 years in our understanding of the relationship between humans and natural systems. Numerous theories have emerged to describe these interactions both in a physical and intellectual sense, such as the socioecological systems theory, the biophilia hypothesis, nature-deficit disorder, deep ecology, ecofeminism, and others. The advancement of technology now enables us to understand biological systems such as DNA and microbial interactions to a degree unimaginable just a few hundred years ago. The amount of data that we understand about biological systems is doubling at least every five years (Rifkin 1999) and likely faster. Natural scientists are now dealing with big data to understand systems-level patterns in ecosystems and the biosphere. School children are learning the interactive principles of ecology and beginning to experience complex systems through the use of the Internet at an early age. Many individuals have transformative experiences in nature that expand their previous notions of humanity and wilderness.

In light of all of this history, today we arrive at shifting conceptions of business as well. The following Table 1.1 summarizes what an ecocentric paradigm means for the business world. While this is a simplistic comparison, it is helpful to demonstrate the big picture of this shift.

The main reason to bring all of this to the forefront is to illuminate that the dominant social narratives of any given era are in constant dialog

Table 1.1 Anthropocentric and ecocentric business paradigms

Epistemology	Anthropocentric perspective	Ecocentric perspective
Philosophical component	Transitional strategies	Transformational strategies
Paradigm	Dominant social paradigm	Ecocentric responsibility paradigm or new ecological paradigm
Value set	Rational Instrumental Egocentric Exemptionalist Narcissistic Economic rationality	Emotional Intrinsic, values-driven Spiritually advanced ecolibrium Empathetic Ecological rationality
Scientific approach	Reductionist Deconstructionist Empirical	Holistic Synthesis Systems-based Homeostatic
Strategy type	Transitional Competitive Continuous improvement Incremental Linear Cradle-to-grave Open-loop Dualistic	Transformational Collaborative, innovative, or visionary Discontinuous Circular Cradle-to-cradle Closed-loop Integrated
Management approach	Eco-efficient Socio-efficient Environmental management, sustainable development, 4Rs—reduce, reuse, recycle, regulate	Eco-effective Socio-effective Ecological sustainability Waste equals food
Marketing strategy	Transitional Incremental Greenwashing Business as usual	Transformational Step change Ecologically sustainable
Overall purpose	Human-centric, business as usual Sustainable development	Ecological sustainability Responsibility for all species and resources
Prospects for the future	Dystopian Destruction is the end game Only choice remaining is the rate of global destruction	Regenerative Restorative Systems-based Productive for business and nature Sustainable global society for all species, with the recognition of the need to reduce human population and consumption

Source: Adapted from Borland and Lindgreen (2012).

with the scientific narratives of that era, shaping one another along the way (Kaye 1997). As we embed complexity and systems sciences into our worldview of the modern era, it enables us to perceive our relationships with each other and with nature differently than previous eras. The afore-mentioned attributes of an emergent ecocentric worldview (Table 1.1) help us differentiate the characteristics of an old paradigm that is dying and a new paradigm that is struggling to be born (as Otto Scharma famously says).

And so it is that *now* is the moment for bioinspiration (and several other ecocentric concepts) to have an audience on a broad public stage, across numerous disciplines. It is a very old idea that has been bubbling below the surface of societal norms, waiting for the right time to emerge. Through our forgetting of our role in nature through time, we have had to reinvent how we conceive our relationship with nature. Bioinspiration is one particularly insightful and, for some, profound approach to this reinvention, and I am grateful to be able to share it with you in this text.

Overview of the Book

Chapter 1 provides an introduction and sets the stage for the dialog herein. Chapter 2 addresses the basics of bioinspiration, including definitions and terms, a discussion of the human relationship to nature, and explores the various ways that bioinspiration can be connected to sustainability. Chapter 3 dives into the application of biological models to management strategies and discusses several examples. Chapter 4 describes how bioin-spiration can be applied to operational decision making. Chapter 5 looks at the various ways that bioinspiration is used in product development processes and discusses some approaches. Chapter 6 zooms out from the organization itself to view the larger surrounding systems of production and consumption as part of a bioinspired innovation strategy. Chapter 7 is dedicated to a collection of tools and processes that are used in corpo-rate and academic settings, and Chapter 8 addresses some of the practical issues with this approach. And finally, Chapter 9 concludes with sugges-tions for further reading and additional resources.

Unlike several existing publications, this book is not intended to be an in-depth conceptual exploration of the philosophy guiding learning from nature, nor does it provide a plethora of existing natural models that you could learn from (e.g., Woolley-Barker 2017) or in-depth case studies of biomimetic companies and technologies (e.g., Harman 2013). Those books have already been written elsewhere (and are available in the *Further Reading* section at the end of the book). While it begins with high-level theory, this book is really more of a tactical and practical introduction to the various approaches and tools that nature-inspired practitioners use. So, put your manager hat on and be prepared to step outside of your usual solution space and into the pine forest, the jungle, or the prairie to guide your team toward a broader understanding of nature, sustainability, and innovation. We will begin with the basics.

CHAPTER 2

The Basics

What Is Bioinspiration?

So, exactly what is bioinspiration? Well, it depends on who you ask. Janine Benyus, an American biologist who coined the term in her 1997 book *Biomimicry: Innovation Inspired by Nature* (Benyus 1997), described it as "the conscious emulation of nature's genius." She said we should view nature as *model, measure, and mentor.* From this perspective, humans are a young, naïve species that simply do not know how to design appropriately for the conditions on earth. Humans are a part of nature, though our communities, infrastructure, and economies are typically erroneously designed as though we are separate from nature. Our design and innovation approaches are clunky and not particularly adept at maintaining functionality for the long haul of life on earth. The source of our environmental challenges is not a moral or ethical one, but is largely one of poor design. We design things that do not perform well in the conditions of the biosphere that support the diversity of life forms that live here, including ourselves. Most other organisms, on the other hand, have been adapting to live on this planet for much longer than we have, and we have a lot to learn from these other organisms about well-adapted design for the conditions on earth. Benyus proposes that we should "create conditions conducive to life" for ourselves and all of the other 30–100 million species that reside on earth with us. Only then will we fully realize the potential of human design and innovation to support humanity. This is the general proposition of bioinspiration, and in some circles, it has come to be known as the *biomimetic promise* (Gleich, Pade, Petschow, and Pissarskoi 2010) that mimicking nature will produce novel, sustainable designs and innovations.

However, while Benyus's book popularized the word as it is known today—connecting learning from nature with sustainability—the

Biomimetic Promise: The common belief that innovations that model natural systems will be inherently novel, better performing, and more sustainable because they are based on natural systems. This represents a naturalist fallacy because it implies that because something is *natural*, it is also *good* without further critical analysis.

predecessors of the concept date back much further. And while these distinctions may seem trivial for managerial needs, there are various schools of related thought that have practical implications for sustainability-oriented innovators. The following section is a brief overview of the history of biologically inspired design and innovation.

Learning from nature is obviously not a new practice. Indeed, our very survival and evolution as a species has been dependent on learning from nature. Many forms of traditional ecological knowledge are based in an intimate connection with natural systems. As an example, the Inuit people of northern North America took cues from polar bears about the appropriate depth, construction, and orientation of their igloo homes. Leonardo Da Vinci took cues from birds when developing his first flying machines (Romei 2008). Even today, the flipped-up tips of airplane wings owe their existence to an engineer's careful observation of soaring birds.

As a specific area of study, bioinspiration emerged when the related terms biomimetics and bionics were first applied to formal research agendas in the mid-1900s. Otto Schmitt is credited with coining the term *biomimetics* in approximately 1969, while Jack Steele coined the term *bionics* in 1958. The primary difference that divides these two camps from each other and from *biomimicry* is the legacy of their origins. While Benyus was a biologist with a strong sustainability message, Schmitt was applying the concept to biomedical applications and Steele was applying it to aerospace engineering. The common thread that links these terms together is the idea of learning from nature. All three terms share the common etymology of bios-, the Ancient Greek word meaning life. Biomimicry and biomimetics share the word—mimesis, meaning *to imitate* and the -*ic* in bionic means *like* or *in the manner of.* In short, all three terms refer to the imitation of biological models for human design and innovation solutions. This application can be metaphorical or analogical (discussed further on page 22), but the premise is the same. Nature is a treasure trove of innovation ideas, many of which humans have never considered, and there is much to be gained from seeking solutions from natural systems.

Today, these terms are frequently used interchangeably, but some subcultures do exist depending on the origins of the user. This is only practically relevant when it relates to the application of bioinspiration for sustainability-oriented innovation. Not all users, with their diverse histories and disciplinary differences, approach bioinspiration with the same sustainability lens, if they apply any sustainability lens whatsoever. In fact, the U.S. Department of Defense is one of the largest funders of biomimetics research, and the sustainability of their endeavors are understandably scrutinized (Johnson 2011). Exactly how to connect bioinspiration to sustainability will be addressed in further detail in later sections, but as an introduction here, it is notable that the discipline-specific origins of different schools of thought influence how various practitioners perceive sustainability.

There are also several related disciplines that are inspired by nature, but have slightly different origins or specific communities of practice. Concepts such as industrial ecology, life cycle analysis, cradle-to-cradle design, and the circular economy are all innovations inspired by nature, though, again their origins are diverse. They too will be discussed in further detail in the following chapters. They are mentioned here to highlight the diversity of applications of this overarching idea of learning from nature.

It may also be helpful to understand what bioinspiration is not. Table 2.1 differentiates between various categories of *bio-innovation* that you may hear about.

For our purposes, bioinspiration will be defined as innovation and design inspired by nature with an intention of enabling humans to become a better-adapted species for life on earth. This definition is loaded with assumptions, and we will aim to unpack some of those assumptions now.

Table 2.1 Biologically related approaches to innovation

Other trendy bio-terms	Loosely defined as	Example
Bioutilization	Using another species directly	Using a maple tree to make a wooden table
Bioassistance	Using another species to produce something that we need	Growing maple trees to harvest maple syrup, but keeping the trees alive
Bioengineering	Translocation of genes from one species to another to add specific genes or traits from other species	Inserting the genes of a maple tree into a pine tree so that pine trees also produce maple syrup (this is a fabricated example, but no stranger than other examples I have heard)
Biomorphic	The translation of biological forms into human artifacts	A building or sculpture, for instance, whose shape is inspired by some aspect of the maple tree's shape
Biophilia	The hypothesis that humans have an innate inclination to seek connection with nature and other forms of life	Planting maple trees in and around our homes because they make us feel calm, engaged, and attuned to the world around us
Biomockery	The abuse of biological models for silly displays of human cleverness	I invented this term, but think of a fried chicken joint that is shaped like an actual chicken
Biomimicry, Biomimetics	The emulation of design principles found in natural systems	The maple tree demonstrates an optimized flow pattern in its leaves, described by Murray's law, and that pattern is applied to the water distribution system (i.e., plumbing) inside of a building

Source: Author.

Business Relationships to Nature

The very idea of learning from nature draws out some interesting questions for users. One of the most pressing issues, from a managerial perspective, is the disconnection in the way we talk about between business and nature. If you are reading this, you are likely a person who takes some interest in the natural world. You likely have some hobbies that take you outdoors (hiking, gardening, etc.). Maybe you were raised in a rural place or on a farm. For whatever reason, you appreciate nature. But have you ever considered your role in nature, as a participant in natural systems?

This is a major component of bioinspiration, and it is quite contrary to the majority of corporate sustainability perspectives. Practicing bioinspiration forces us to address any assumptions we may hold about whether humans are part of nature or separate from it. While the economic drivers of business force us to think of nature in terms of supply chains and raw materials, we often overlook the very real and tangible implications that these decisions have on the biosphere. This is generally not something done intentionally. For many people raised in a Western perspective of nature, philosophy, and religion, humans are not a part of nature. Nature is something that is out there—to be feared, revered, or preserved in wilderness areas. Nature is not something within us and around us in our cities and homes. We are not animals, and we are not subject to the same laws of nature that all of the other organisms are. Or are we?

The various ways that we perceive our relationship to nature in different contexts influence many aspects of our decision making in our personal and professional lives. Most of us would teach our children to pick up litter on a forest trail in a national park, as we view stewardship of a pristine natural place as a high priority. Concurrently, however, we may be faced with business decisions that force us to choose between our ecological ethic and supply chain viability. Do we choose to source recycled plastic that costs more, potentially compromising the market viability of our product? Or, do we source virgin plastic that drives habitat destruction and water pollution, but ensures that our business and livelihood are sustained? Or is there some middle ground that we can identify? The sustainability-minded professional is faced with these types of difficult decisions on a regular basis. Our behavior in these two scenarios is inextricably linked to the ways that we perceive society (i.e., ourselves), nature (e.g., protected national parks, rural mining sites, our backyard habitats, etc.), and business (i.e., the mechanisms that allow us to create value to sustain ourselves in the modern economy). And frequently, our perceptions of society, nature, and business change depending on the contexts that we find ourselves in. The *me* in a national park behaves differently than the *me* sitting behind my computer. Let us consider the following conceptions of the relationship between nature, business, and society that are common in business literature (Marcus, Kurucz, and Colbert 2010).

The first model, described as the disparate model (Figure 2.1), positions nature and society as separate and exogenous entities from business.

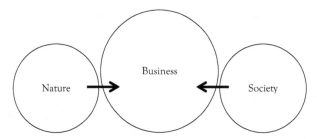

Figure 2.1 The disparate model

Source: Adapted from Marcus, Kurucz, and Colbert (2010).

In this model, nature is not seen as having a major influence on business decisions, and the decisions that we make in supply chains are not directly related to the health of ecological systems. This view tends to lend itself to technocentric approaches to sustainability challenges and caters to the belief that the economy alone can solve environmental and social problems.

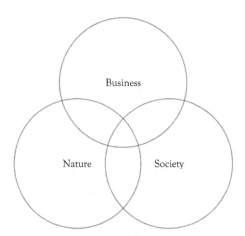

Figure 2.2 The intertwined model

Source: Adapted from Marcus, Kurucz, and Colbert (2010).

The second model, described as the intertwined model (Figure 2.2), gives equal importance to nature, society, and business. This is frequently referred to as the Triple Bottom Line (Elkington 1997) and proposes that all three aspects are critical to decision making concurrently and with equal magnitude. In this framing, the three components are mutually enhancing for one another, and trade-offs among benefits to each aspect are frequently necessary in decision making. Ecological systems are influential for and influenced by business and society, but the three factors are not necessarily or by default interdependent or causally linked.

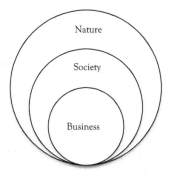

Figure 2.3 The embedded model

Source: Adapted from Marcus, Kurucz, and Colbert (2010).

The third model, the embedded model (Figure 2.3), positions business as inseparable from nature and society, with them being related in a nested way. All human activity is inextricably embedded in ecological systems, and business is represented as one aspect of society. The embedded model posits that society is dependent on nature, and business is, therefore, dependent on its embeddedness in society and nature. This perspective, while common among natural scientists, is rare among business scholars and professionals. When asked, many people would say: "Of course humans are a part of nature." This model seems obvious and intuitive at first glance. But concurrently, the same individuals would make decisions based on the underlying assumptions of the other two models, without necessarily considering that their mental frame has shifted. And this mental shift has consequences for ecological systems.

The primary reason for presenting these three conceptions is to acknowledge that, for humans to successfully pursue any type of sustainability-oriented innovation, bioinspired or otherwise, we need to perceive ourselves as being embedded in ecological systems. We need to acknowledge and consider that we—and our technologies—are participants in the biophysical cycles that define life on earth. We must become apperceptive

participants in ecological systems and biophysical cycles in our every decision. Apperceptive participants are quite simply participants who know
that they are participating and make decisions accordingly. And now that
you are privy to these models, you too are an apperceptive participant
making conscious decisions about how you interact with nature. Now let
us discuss some terminology related to the quality of this participation.

Sustainability, Resilience, and Regeneration

Terms related to sustainability are as subject to fashion as anything else
in modern society. Particularly in the fast-paced world of digital media,
it is easy for new trends and memes to gain traction at lightning speed
without significant, thoughtful development of context and meaning. It
is easy to brush off the distinctions among terms, as our brains tend to
associate new concepts with existing concepts that we are already familiar with. But words matter and the differences between concepts matter,
even if we are able to tell ourselves that a new concept is just like one
that we already know. For this reason, we will discuss three terms that are
frequently used interchangeably in the context of corporate social responsibility: sustainability, resilience, and regeneration.

Sustainability and relatedly, sustainable development are the most recognized terms associated with the modern corporate social responsibility.
According to one researcher, sustainability had more than 300 definitions
when he surveyed the academic literature nearly 20 years ago (Dobson
1998). According to the most commonly cited definition, "Sustainable
development is development that meets the needs of the present without compromising the ability of future generations to meet their own
needs" (World Commission on Environment and Development 1987).
This broad definition has been applied to many different contexts and
in various ways. The definition that I am personally most fond of is this:
"Sustainability is the possibility that humans and other life will flourish
on Earth forever" (Ehrenfeld 2008). On the other hand, in some circles,
the root word *sustain* implies that we are trying to sustain existing conditions or create businesses that are sustainable without the larger context
of the sustainability of society and nature. Similar to biomimetics, I bring
these terms to the forefront to bring attention to our own biases and the
assumptions that we bring to the table.

> **What is Sustainability?**
> Take a moment to make a few notes for yourself. What does sustainability mean to you? How do you think about it differently in your personal and professional lives? What actions do you take that demonstrate these different perceptions?

Sustainability is also used in the context of sustainability-oriented innovation. Adams et al. (Adams, Jeanrenaud, Bessant, Denyer, and Overy 2016) define sustainability-oriented innovation as "making intentional changes to an organization's philosophy and values, as well as to its products, processes or practices, to serve the specific purpose of creating and realizing social and environmental value in addition to economic returns" (p. 2). Notice that this definition emphasizes philosophy and values at the forefront and the physical stuff of the organization, the "products, processes and practices" as an additional component to a sustainability-oriented innovation approach. In short, sustainability-oriented innovation is not just about developing green products to sell to consumers or developing new marketing channels for existing products that could be viewed as environmentally friendly. It is about changing the role of business in society toward not only creating economic value for the company, its employees, and shareholders, but also creating novel sources of value for society and ecological systems at the same time. These distinctions are important when considering the various applications of bioinspiration for sustainability-oriented innovation.

Resilience is another term that has become common in recent years, particularly as the realities of climate change begin to become obvious to management professionals. Unlike sustainability and sustainable development, which emerged from the perspective of the social sciences, resilience is a concept that was first applied to ecological systems. In the natural sciences, resilience refers to the capacity of a system to maintain functionality in the midst of—and recover after—a disturbance event. Notice there are subtle differences from the commonly used definitions that come to mind referring to the ability to bounce back after setbacks, adapt to change, and persevere in the face of adversity. Although these characteristics are similar and related, it is an important distinction that they are, indeed, different. The maintaining of functionality suggests that disturbances are integrated into operations, rather than viewed as disruptive invaders to otherwise well-oiled machines. This is particularly relevant in the application of bioinspiration, when companies are aiming to *be like nature* and embody the characteristics of natural systems. Resilience is one of the principles of life that we will discuss in more detail next, but for the time being, let us distinguish it as conceptually complimentary to, but distinct from, sustainability.

A final related term, regeneration, is also emerging as an approach to innovation and corporate social responsibility. The definitions of regeneration are variable, with applications in medicine, engineering, biology, chemistry, agriculture, and design. For our purposes, we will rely heavily on regeneration as defined in the design world. In this definition, a regenerative design is based on a systems ecology approach with an end goal of redeveloping systems that enable the co-evolution of humans as part of a diverse community of thriving species. It involves closed-loop systems of input and output that result in a net positive effect for socioecological systems. This has implications for business operations, and a few examples of this in a corporate context will be provided in later sections. Although the terms are frequently used interchangeably in conversation, the definition is provided here as a distinction from both sustainability and resilience.

As you can see, the world of corporate social responsibility is subject to trends like any other aspect of society. While accountability is an important aspect of corporate social responsibility strategies that we frequently rely on, annual sustainability reports only get us so far. Sustainability, resilience, and regeneration have distinctly different meanings, and our intentions are shaped by the way we apply these concepts in our day-to-day practices. These terms also influence how we gauge the efficacy of biomimetic innovation. The terminology that we use to guide annual reports has significant impact on the things that we monitor and measure, and consequently, how we perceive our progress toward a society that serves all 30–100 million species that live on planet earth.

We can consider these terms somewhere on a gradient of possible innovation scenarios that includes destructive (or degenerative), sustainable, resilient, regenerative, and flourishing (Figure 2.4). Destructive or regenerative approaches to innovation are not necessarily intended to be so, but destruction of ecological and social systems is a by-product of design, development, and innovation. This is often due to externalities or waste in systems of production and consumption. An example of this might be destruction of forests to clear land for mining activities and the mine tailings that cause disruptions to living systems for several generations. A goal of a sustainability agenda might aim to consider the ecological and social implications as equally important as the economic factors in an innovation project. For instance, Patagonia is an American outdoor apparel company that has developed very effective systems for comparing the sustainability of various production methods. They pay close attention to the conditions for workers in their factories and how their operations influence the surrounding ecosystems. They choose factories, designs, materials, and dyes with all of these factors in mind. In terms of resilience, it is frankly quite difficult to discern what resilience means in a corporate context, and for me to easily identify a resilient company example. This is largely because the socioecological conditions of our time are only really beginning to shift. While the economic downturn of 2008 represented a disturbance on one level, we have yet to see major disruptions in supply chains and distribution channels on a global scale. A smaller-scale example of resilience might be a clothing company whose primary suppliers are in the Middle East and crops suffer due to severe drought or civil unrest disrupts production. This company demonstrates resilience when it finds another source of cotton in a more stable region. As I will describe in a later chapter, regenerative companies actively seek to use their organizations for net positive impact by restoring the socioecological system functionality. An example of this might be to recover junk metal from a public landfill to be reincorporated into supply chains

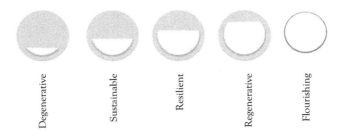

Figure 2.4 Shifting sustainability narratives

Source: Author.

for new cars. And finally, thriving societies and companies are those in which restored socioecological systems are maintained in balance at their optimal performance. They are not just living, not just surviving, but rather, they are flourishing and getting satisfaction from the lives, livelihoods, and communities they engage with through time. You can visual this transition with the following gradient (Figure 2.4).

As we progress into the next chapters of the book, keep these distinctions in mind. The examples of bioinspiration given herein and those that you come across in your daily activities will exemplify one of the aforementioned characteristics and frequently, more than one at the same time. The important thing, as a practitioner of bioinspiration, is to develop sensitivity to our intentionality as an innovator. While we may not achieve the ideal outcomes for bioinspiration, with a perfected approach to emulating natural systems, we can begin to use a critical eye about our intentions and progress by becoming familiar with a diversity of perspectives.

Metaphor Versus Analogy

Another issue that frequently goes overlooked in the application of bioinspiration is the difference between metaphor and analogy. While biology can be an immense source of fodder for innovation, the way that fodder gets applied can be very literal or very figurative. While we often use the terms metaphor and analogy interchangeably, there are distinctions that are relevant when determining how biological concepts get applied to design. John Ehrenfeld, a sustainability scholar who frequently writes about learning from nature, summarized the differences rather well:

> Analogy is a practical notion that compares two cases and suggests an alternative way of addressing the situation facing an actor in the first case, based on the presumption that the same rules apply as in the second case. Analogy is a kind of map and is useful for solving normal problems by transforming the situation confronting the actor to another, familiar scene.
>
> Simile or metaphor is a figure of speech that is suggestive and transformative. It is not a map as is an analogy. It enables a

problem solver or artist to escape from the rules that constrain routine action, that is, acts that take place within established cognitive and cultural beliefs and norms. In contrast to the [...] definition for analogy, metaphor does not assume the often-erroneous logic that if things are alike in some sense, they are alike in others. As noted, metaphors are only suggestive. Analogies are often used prescriptively and can lead to false conclusions and mistakes in practice by assuming that because one thing follows another, it must be because of the prior act (post hoc, ergo propter hoc), an ancient bugaboo of logicians.

Thinking of industrial systems as ecological systems in metaphorical terms may hatch learning and creative acts without establishing that the two systems are analogous, that is, following the same rules. For example, one can invoke the notion of interconnectedness, closed loops, community, local sufficiency, or diversity as qualitative (metaphorical) similarities without claiming that materials and energy flow through industrial networks according to the same rules as ecosystems. It may be that there are indeed analogies between the two, but these need to be established through scientific observation. A metaphor is never wrong or incorrect; it is only useful or not. An analogy may be objectively false. (Ehrenfeld 2003, pp. 1–2)

These distinctions are an important aspect of bioinspiration that are generally overlooked. The biomimetic promise would lead us to believe that because a technology mimics nature, it is inherently *better* than its predecessors. But Ehrenfeld's point about the analogical transfer of a biological concept, this transfer should be prescriptive, including a contextual relevance. What we frequently find in bioinspired innovation is a metaphorical transfer of biological strategy that is inspirational and useful in a creative process, but not necessarily biologically accurate. The difficult job of the bioinspired practitioner is to uphold rigorous standards of biological accuracy at the same time as developing innovative solutions. A successful practitioner can map their thought processes from biology-to-design or challenge-to-biology with accuracy and recognition of where they are using analogy and where they are relying on metaphor.

Bioinspiration + Sustainability

After six years as a full-time biomimicry consultant and over a year into my PhD research, I was still struggling to understand exactly how bioinspiration was connected to corporate social responsibility and sustainability-oriented innovation. I had read as much literature as I could get my hands on, scouring for patterns and distinctions among the diverse bodies of theory. However, there is an underlying issue at play that I failed to recognize early on. Part of the disconnect between the application of biological models to sustainability challenges lies in the motivations and intentions of various disciplinary approaches. As Alexandra Daisy Ginsberg summarizes, "The designer is better equipped as a generalist, in contrast to the scientist, who is a specialist, an expert in the detail of how things work, not whom they work for" (Ginsberg, Calvert, Schyfter, Eflick, and Endy 2014, p. 45). In this commentary lies the heart of the issue in connecting biology, design, and sustainability. When we approach questions of sustainability, we must address the issue of who will win and lose in the process of innovation. The direct translation of biological strategy into innovative outcomes does not necessarily ask questions of right and wrong, win and lose. It simply begs questions of *based-on-biology* or *not-based-on-biology*. To expand this conversation space to the realm of sustainability is to open a Pandora's box of perspectives, debates, certifications, and personal convictions.

Although several attempts have been made among various academics and consultants to clearly connect bioinspiration to sustainability, I found little satisfying result that was applicable across scales. So, after months of reading, writing, discussing, and fretting, I decided to ask users themselves via an exploratory online survey. I eventually got responses from over 70 bioinspired practitioners, ranging from biologists to designers to engineers to business people. Their responses were as diverse as their interests, but a few general patterns emerged. Most practitioners were coming from one of the three perspectives when connecting bioinspiration and sustainability: 1) they focused on the elemental and inherent sustainability principles of natural systems; 2) they were strongly influenced by the sociological origins of sustainable development; or, 3) they approached sustainability from the quantitative contributions of earth sciences. There were also a few other discipline-specific approaches that will be briefly discussed at the end of this section.

Perspectives Connecting Bioinspiration and Sustainability Among Various Practitioners:

1. **Life is Sustainable:** Life is inherently sustainable, and if we mimic all the principles of living systems, we will be sustainable too.

2. **The Three Pillars:** Bioinspiration should be used to enable sustainable development with consideration of the three pillars of sustainability—the social, the ecological, and the economic. This is often referred to as the *Triple Bottom Line**.

3. **Science-Based Targets:** The dynamics of socioecological systems and consequently, human sustainability and resilience, can be measured against earth science datasets, and biosinpiration should be accountable to science-based metrics.

---

*Triple Bottom Line is attributed to Elkington (1997).

Source: Adapted from Mead and Jeanrenaud 2017.

Is Life Inherently Sustainable?

The most common approach and the reason that many people are attracted to bioinspiration are the ideas that nature is inherently sustainable, and nature's designs are time-tested for success via the processes of evolution. It seems obvious and intuitive, at first glance. So, let us spend some time unpacking what is meant by the guiding principles of ecological systems.

The same basic forces and laws shape all of life on earth. Sunlight, water, and gravity are unique to earth (from what we know with certainty), and they are the defining features that have enabled life to flourish. The second law of thermodynamics says that entropy (or the tendency toward disorder) is always increasing through time. Life, however, uses various forms of energy to fight entropy and maintain homeostasis (or a balanced state) required for survival. When living things get too far away from this balanced state, that is when systems start to fail. Living organisms are always responding to cycles, seasons, and rhythms created by the rotation of the planets. Summer, winter, fall, spring. Day and night. Tides rising and falling. Benyus (1997) framed the following nine principles in her book:

Benyus's Principles of Nature

- Nature runs on sunlight.
- Nature uses only the energy it needs.
- Nature fits form to function.
- Nature recycles everything.
- Nature rewards cooperation.
- Nature banks on diversity.
- Nature demands local expertise.
- Nature curbs excesses from within.
- Nature taps the power of limits.

Through time with her consultancy work, Benyus and her colleagues at Biomimicry 3.8 (myself included) went on to create this more elaborate assemblage of Life's Principles™ with considerably more detail intended as a design guide for bioinspired innovation projects.

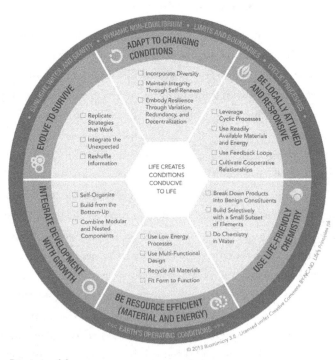

Source: Biomimicry 3.8.

These principles, derived from several bodies of theory in chemistry, ecology, evolutionary biology, and physics, explain the majority of evolutionary and adaptive processes of Life (with a capital L, meaning all of the organisms on the earth). This is a robust collection of concepts that has been tailored for a wide array of audiences. Biomimics frequently refer to these principles in their daily activities in small and big ways. It is a helpful tool in a biomimetic innovation process for sustainability.

Proponents of the biomimetic promise assert that, if we follow all of these principles in the design of human systems, our designs will be inherently sustainable as well. Trouble is, you see, that we rarely have the opportunity to apply *all* of these principles to one innovation project because our scale of influence is limited by our role. So, while the application of these principles may seem obvious and intuitive for sustainability-oriented innovation, there are numerous critiques from natural scientists to challenge this assumption.

For instance, it has been noted that natural systems strive for sufficiency, rather than efficiency, meaning that they aim to meet the lowest possible operational standards without expending excessive energy. In many cases, sufficient design is not the most efficient possibility and the technological inclination to seek efficient solutions often overrides the acceptance of sufficiency.

There are also issues of time scales for sustainability. We are typically designing for time scales that reflect somewhere within the human life span, whereas Life has been evolving its design strategies for 3.8 billion years. When we approach design for sustainability, over what time frames? How many generations? What ecological and social contexts?

Additionally, biological strategy is uniquely designed for a particular ecological context and optimized for specific characteristics. When taken out of context, the same biological strategy is not necessarily the most effective. As Alexandra Daisy Ginsberg writes, "Biology is being remodeled into a design discipline in the name of progress, but progress and evolution follow different rules ... Evolution responds to context, not intention."

As an example of these conundrums, I once worked on the design of a commercial building located on the front range of the Rocky Mountains. Prairie dogs, small burrowing mammals, are common inhabitants of this region and as such, we decided to investigate how they were building their underground homes to manage the ambient winds for passive ventilation. And while prairie dogs are optimizing for passive ventilation, their burrows also serve other functions such as storing food, chambers for sleeping, and spaces to protect and rear young. All of these functions were designed for simultaneously. However, given how well-developed passive ventilation strategies were in the built environment and the fact that the architects were attempting to maximize passive ventilation, they were skeptical that the prairie dog had much to teach them.

For me, this story exemplifies a few key messages. First, when decontextualized, not all biological strategies may provide useful insights. Second, it is difficult to justify relying on biological strategies when existing engineered strategies are already quite effective. Third, in-depth research into biological strategies can be incredibly difficult to accomplish within the timeframe and budgets of commercial projects. And finally, humans need to have the humility to consider the possibility that we might not have the most effective solutions and that we could have something to learn from ecological systems. Janine Benyus refers to this as *quieting our cleverness*, and it is a skill that we can all benefit from learning.

> ***Quieting Our Cleverness:*** An expression coined by Janine Benyus to describe the necessary personal and cognitive transition when using bioinspiration. This approach requires that we move from solving problems based on our existing knowledge to solving problems based on nature's strategies. In practice with an innovation team, this requires that we defer judgment, expand the potential solution space, identify unlikely leverage points, and take the time to consider novel and even radical approaches.

While I have laid out several critiques of the concept of learning from nature, I still, after 20 years involved in both social and ecological aspects of sustainability, believe that bioinspiration is the single most powerful concept that we have to address the socioecological challenges that lie before us. These critiques (and numerous others) deserve consideration and provide insights into what motivates people to make changes for sustainability. Listening to rival ideas and doubts is perhaps the most effective entry point to overcoming them in any context, and bioinspiration is no exception. With that caveat, I will give my opinion that Life is not, in fact, inherently sustainable. But it is a lot closer to sustainable than industrial development has been in the last 200 years, and we have a lot to learn about how to live on this planet of ours.

Connecting With the Sustainable Development and Earth Science Communities

Returning to my survey results, many users rely on approaches that were common in their disciplines that have evolved as a result of ongoing dialog related to sustainable development. For many, this means considering the three pillars of sustainability or the triple bottom line—the intertwined social, economic, and ecological aspects of sustainability. From this perspective, sustainability is largely a consideration of human agents acting in a world that is constructed by our actions, beliefs, and values. Our relationships with each other and with nature are a reflection of our values. It is the value of all forms of Life that drives our decision making for sustainability, guided by moral and ethical responsibility, and stewardship of society and nature. The most recent major influence in this conversation, preceded by the Millennium Development Goals, has been the Sustainable Development Goals (often referred to as SDGs) developed by the United Nations. These high-level goals create a visionary framework for what sustainable societies look like and leave the operational or policy guidelines up to governing bodies. Monitoring and measuring tools related to this view include: The Global Reporting Initiative (mostly social with some ecological aspects); ISO 14000 Series standards for environmental performance (mostly ecological aspects), LEED and BREEAM Standards in the built environment (social and environmental aspects), and other standardized approaches that are applied in various contexts. This entry point seemed to be more common among social scientists and business types, though they also used other approaches as well. There were also a few people who commented more intuitive interpretations of sustainability.

Other (typically natural scientists) users focus heavily on the perspectives of the earth sciences, resilience science, and the interactions between social and natural systems as indicators of success in the application of bioinspiration. Much of the most current work in this area is coming out of the Stockholm Resilience Center and their work identifying Planetary Boundaries for a *safe operating space for humanity.*

Planetary Boundaries: A Safe Operating Space for Humanity

1. Climate change
2. Ocean acidification
3. Stratospheric ozone depletion
4. Nitrogen and phosphorous cycling
5. Global freshwater use
6. Change in land use
7. Biodiversity loss
8. Atmospheric aerosol loading
9. Chemical pollution

For these users, the sustainability of innovation efforts should be viewed within the boundaries of the earth's carrying capacity and the ability of ecological systems to maintain functionality in spite of the stressors created by human development activities. These users rely heavily on data-driven perspectives related to corporate social responsibility and sustainability-oriented innovation. Measuring and monitoring is based on resource use in real terms, without proxies created by external monitoring agencies. While there is a growing group of businesses becoming interested in this approach (e.g., the World Business Council for Sustainable Development), it is yet to be seen how the limits to growth inherent in ecological systems will be reconciled with a global economy driven by growth.

Concluding Remarks

There are various other approaches to connect sustainability and bioinspiration, with more created on a regular basis (see examples in *Further Reading*). There is ultimately no right or wrong approach to connect bioinspiration to sustainability-oriented innovation. In fact, most practitioners applied a combination of approaches as was demanded of their industry standards, clients, customers, and regulatory bodies. And many practitioners relied on less tangible indicators such as intuition and the changes of perception of their clients. What is necessary, however, is to approach a biologically inspired innovation process with the same critical eye and rigor that we would in any innovation process and to resist falling into the trap of assuming that something intended to be like nature actually is. It took Life 3.8 million years to get us here and we still have a lot to learn. Thankfully, 30–100 million other species have been learning along with us, and given the opportunity, they will teach us a lot about how to be well-adapted to this planet of ours.

CHAPTER 3

Innovations in Management

For most managers, one of their primary concerns—in addition to the solvency of the business—is the way that they interact with employees. And given the proliferation of management consultants, there are certainly a lot of ideas out there about how that should be done. Taking a bird's eye view on our organizations, we tend to create elaborate pyramid structures that facilitate ease of assignment of workload, and probably more importantly, mechanisms of accountability. But there are also numerous organizations dating back to the 1950s that have thrown hierarchies to the wind in favor of strategies that emulate natural systems. We will discuss a few success stories in this chapter and provide some biological fodder for consideration for future management innovations.

Let us spend a moment differentiating management innovations from operational- or enterprise-level innovations. Management innovations specifically target the act of management and the organizational structures and concepts that support managing. You have probably heard of Lean or Total Quality Management. These are two examples of management innovations that focus specifically on incremental efficiency improvements and quality as a primary objective. In a similar way, biological models have been used to inform organizational communication strategies, set priorities, and plan for growth.

We will provide an overview here and give you few tidbits in case you would like to try it for yourself. We will start with those organizations that view bioinspiration as a visionary tool for sustainability-oriented innovation, and then, get into some other models that are loosely directed at organizational sustainability, but are generally more inwardly focused than they are focused on the sustainability of socioecological systems.

Nature is THE Standard for Sustainability

What does it mean to be like nature? This is a question that plagued my PhD research and continues to haunt me today—in the most provocative way possible. Come to find out, there are a few organizations grappling with this question too. Throughout the rest of the book, I will refer to two organizations that have dug their heels in to answer this question. For these organizations, sustainability is equated with bioinspiration, and bioinspiration is interwoven into their sustainability, innovation, and business strategies. The very question of learning from nature, for them, signifies a quieting of our cleverness (as Benyus says) in their overall approach to management. This big idea of innovating to be like nature has many different effects throughout the organization, and we will come back to several of the many outcomes of this innovation strategy throughout the rest of the text. To look at this specifically as a management innovation, it means that these organizations use nature's strategies as their primary standard for what is sustainable and what is not. This is in addition to the industry standards and certifications that are common for their industries. Without overselling (because we are all works in progress), these organizations exemplify to what it means to do the work of following the principles of life.

The first, rather famous, case that is worth mentioning is the story of Interface Carpets. This story has been done from many different angles, so apologies if this seems like old news. However, since their founder Ray Anderson's death, their story and his legacy only continue to grow, so this is a story worth staying current on. If you talk to nearly anyone who has been at Interface for a while, they immediately soften when they talk about Ray's vision for the company. They describe how in the mid-1990s, Ray had an epiphany about his industrialist impact on the world after reading Paul Hawken's book, *The Ecology of Commerce*. With his newfound knowledge that his company was one of many in the business of take–make–waste product life cycles, he decided that he would completely re-envision the company, and in the process, drive broader changes in the carpet industry. This began their "climb up Mount Sustainability," as Ray describes it in a few of his own autobiographical books. As part of this sustainability overhaul, Ray assembled a sort of *green dream team* of sustainability experts who served as sherpas for Interface, guiding them up the mountain. This climb up involved many different approaches to sustainability-oriented innovation, and bioinspiration was strongly influential. At the time, Benyus (a member of the dream team) had just written *Biomimicry: Innovation Inspired by Nature*, and the principles of nature mentioned in the first chapter (Nature runs on sunlight, Nature uses only the energy that it needs, etc.) were instrumental in shaping the re-direction of the company. Interface now refers to Biomimicry 3.8's larger set of Life's Principles to guide their path. These principles serve as a detailed checklist of life-centered criteria to integrate into various organizational endeavors related to sustainability and innovation. Today, they are recognizable in many different innovations that will be discussed in more detail later.

Ecover is a second organization that has adopted this goal of being like nature in their long-term innovation strategy. While they are still in the early days of this exploration compared to Interface's 20-year process, they have the advantage of an embedded sustainability culture since their inception. As a company, Ecover was specifically created to address a need in the deep green cleaning market, and they have continued to expand since their inception. Historically, they were focused on what was inside the bottle (i.e., green cleaning products), and throughout the development of the company, they have become progressively more engaged in the entire life cycle of their products and the overall participation of the company in socioecological systems. Like Interface, they currently have several ongoing bioinspired projects that will also be discussed in subsequent chapters.

These organizations share a few common characteristics. First, the companywide culture of sustainability and innovation is an aspirational one. The senior leadership is engaged in using the company's business strategy to have a net positive impact on society. While they do measure their impact, it is not only a sense of corporate responsibility that drives their sustainability activities but rather, it is the larger vision to use business as a driver for social and ecological benefit that motivates them.

So, as we touched on in the introduction chapter, the application of biological inspiration can take many different forms related to sustainability. For Interface and Ecover, bioinspiration is a management innovation to signpost their journey toward sustainability. Other organizations also use biological models to shed light on efficiency, resilience, cooperation, and other managerial concerns, but the end game for these organizations is more internally focused. The next section provides a few examples of how organizations are utilizing biological models for other aspects of management.

Swarm Theory: The Other Lessons From the Birds and the Bees

Perhaps you have wondered how a flock of birds can circle and swoop in close proximity, without ever colliding into each other. Or maybe you have noticed how ants seem to know where to go for food in a steady, orderly stream, without any one individual leading the.way. These behaviors and those found in other species such as bees, fish, bacteria, locusts, herding animals, and yes, even humans in crowds, can be described as swarming or herd behaviors. Swarm behaviors are guided by a set of simple rules that all members of a group abide by that enable complex behaviors to emerge. For instance, a flock of starlings (called a murmuration) is able to engage in fast and complex movement patterns because each individual knows the rules. Stay within a particular speed range. Stay a particular distance from the individual flying next to me. And done—complex behavior.(*Biologists note: There is clearly more going on biochemically, physiologically, and socially than this ridiculously simplified version, but you get the point. If you have never seen a murmuration, definitely worth a quick search for some video footage. Fantastic spectacle!) Here are few examples of companies that have embraced the simple rules mantra with great success.

Southwest Airlines, for instance, has been taking cues from ants to create greater efficiency in their operations in a couple of ways. When ants are searching for food, they divide themselves into two groups: the scouts and the gatherers. The scouts are primarily responsible for laying down pheromone trails that tell the gatherers the most efficient routes to get the food. As more ants go to the same source, the pheromone trails get stronger and the less efficient trails fade away, resulting in an optimized, highly efficient search pattern. Southwest Airlines began applying some of these types of optimization strategies to their cargo shipping logistics and boarding processes and found more efficient results for themselves. The first example, succinctly described by Eric Bonabeau and Christopher Meyer, addressed an issue they were having with moving cargo between locations. Bonabeau and Meyer write:

> A little more than a year ago, Southwest Airlines was having trouble with its cargo operations. Even though the average plane was using only 7% of its cargo space at some airports there wasn't enough capacity to accommodate scheduled loads of freight, leading to bottlenecks throughout Southwest's cargo routing and handling system. At the time, employees were trying to load freight onto the first plane going in the right direction—a seemingly reasonable strategy. But because of it, workers were spending an unnecessary amount of time moving cargo around and sometimes filling aircraft needlessly. To solve its problem, Southwest turned to an unlikely source: ants. Specifically, researchers looked at the way ants forage, using simple rules, always finding efficient routes to food sources. When they applied this research to Southwest's problem, they discovered something surprising: it can be better to leave cargo on a plane headed initially in the wrong direction. If, for example, they wanted to send a package from Chicago to Boston, it might actually be more efficient to leave it on a plane heading for Atlanta and then Boston than to take if off and put it on the next flight to Boston.
>
> Applying this insight has slashed freight transfer rates by as much as 80% at the busiest cargo stations, decreased the workload for the people who move cargo by as much as 20%, and dramatically reduced the number of overnight transfers. [...] Thanks to the improvements, Southwest estimates an annual gain of more than $10 million. (Bonabeau and Meyer 2001, p.108)

Southwest Airlines has also applied this same ant logic to test their unassigned seating process for efficiency and found it to be relatively optimized. According to swarm theory experts, social insects are so good at what they do, dominating life on earth, because of three main characteristics. First, as a group, they have the flexibility to adapt to a changing environment. Second, they are robust because, when one or a few individuals fail, the rest of the group can pick up the slack and still maintain overall performance of the group. And third, they are self-organized with neither local supervision nor central control. These principles, transferrable to management, are quite contradictory to the mostly top-down, command-and-control type structures that we are accustomed too. While the idea of self-organization may be tough to swallow for a business executive who spent his life building a company from the ground up, it is ultimately self-organization that causes flexibility and robustness (Bonabeau and Meyer 2001).

Another organization that borrows some principles of swarm theory, though they do not outwardly acknowledge using bioinspiration, is WL Gore and Associates, the makers of numerous hi-tech materials and most famously, Gore-Tex™. Gore is composed of Associates, rather than employees, who agree to company wide and individual *commitments* (not assignments) to guide their work—suspiciously similar to simple rules, no? Communication channels are achieved through a *lattice*, rather than through a hierarchy. Though the organization is not totally flat, with some designated leadership, these leaders usually emerge via a nomination from *followers* who view them as sources of support and representative voices of the company. Once a particular factory location reaches 200 people, they branch off to form a new location where a close and personal communication can still flourish amongst a small group—a trait of many social species.

An additional resource *The BioTeaming Manifesto* (freely available on the Web) summarizes some of the most successful attributes of *living teams* into principles to guide team interactions and performance outcomes. They propose seven beliefs necessary for what they call *High Performance Teams*.

These authors stress that a structural change to an organization without an accompanying strategy for managing the necessary cultural changes will be of little success. They promote the use of beliefs, values, and commitments to drive the structure of an organization, shaping its simple rules.

> **Seven Beliefs of BioTeams**
> - Clear and public accountability
> - Trusted competency
> - Give and take
> - Total transparency
> - Shared glory
> - Meaningful mission value
> - Outcome optimism

Source: Thompson and Good (2005).

Chaordic Organizations

Although the ecological and biological systems around us generally seem to be stable, there are actually constant forces at play that maintain a balance between chaos and order. Any complex dynamic system such as flocks of birds, schools of fish, and swarms of locusts are concurrently demonstrating intricately coordinated behavior guided by a few simple rules at the same time that they are balancing the forces of entropy, which create an inherent tendency toward disorder. It is the balancing of forces that makes them both fragile and resilient. These kinds of systems have been coined as *chaordic systems* by an unlikely theorist—retired financial executive.

One of the first modern organizational biomimics is someone who turned the financial world on its head in the 1960s and someone you have probably never heard of. Dee Hock was the driving force behind the creation of the Visa Corporation, which, today, is probably the most prolific financial brand in the world. But who owns Visa? We all have Visa cards, but we do not make payments to Visa. How is it that nearly every retailer in the world has access to its payment channels—from the largest global chains of fast food restaurants in Hong Kong or Paris, to the smallest, mobile-equipped roadside stand in Central America? The Visa brand is everywhere, thanks to the intentional design based on the balance of chaos and order found in natural systems. After years of reading and studying complexity in systems (e.g., biological systems), Hock was charged with creating a mechanism for the global exchange of value as the chair of a group of bankers aiming to solve issues with the existing credit structure. After an intensive process, they came up with several principles to guide the creation of this system including: equitable ownership by all participants; maximization of distributed power, function, and governance; infinite malleability while maintaining a high level of durability; and the ability to attract a diversity of people and institutions that are adaptable to constantly changing conditions. While these principles relate specifically to a human system, these same concepts are quite evident in the principles of High Performance Teams and swarms as described by the aforementioned authors. The twist with the Visa Corporation is that Hock gave a new name to this way of managing complexity. He coined the term *chaordic* to describe the narrow space between chaos and order where living systems thrive—at the other end of the spectrum compared to the illusion of control that we typically try to impose on our organizations (Hock and Senge 2009).

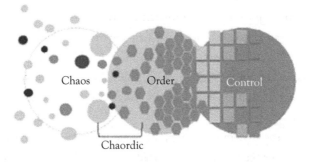

Source: Adapted from the Chaordic Commons.

Business Ecosystems

One final example of a biologically inspired management innovation is the concept of a business ecosystem. Rather than viewing an organization as an isolated entity, several authors have proposed that managers should position their organizations as one of several businesses in a business ecosystem. This business ecosystem is composed of a loose network of suppliers, distributors, technology providers, producers of related products and services, and other types of organizations that a company interacts with. In their book, *The Keystone Advantage*, Iansiti and Levien (Iansiti and Levien 2004) argue that companies need to position themselves as the keystone species in their business ecosystem. In an ecosystem, a keystone species is an organism that has a disproportionately large effect on its environment relative to its abundance. The authors translate a keystone company slightly differently, but with some similar qualities. They stress the importance of a keystone company to improve the overall health of the ecosystem and promote that a keystone company can increase the overall productivity of the entire business ecosystem, creating more abundance for everyone. They advocate that a keystone species brings greater robustness to the overall system by creating a more stable environment for all participants. And finally, they point out that the removal of this species is catastrophic for the entire ecosystem.

This perspective can be a helpful model, and the ideas proposed in the book have gained substantial traction in the business literature. As a manager, you likely refer to your business ecosystem these days. However, as a biologist, I would like to point out a few inconsistencies in the use of this metaphor. First, several of the attributes that conveniently fit with the business world are not necessarily consistent with what we find in ecological systems. They do get it right that keystone species have a disproportionate effect on the other participants in the ecosystem. However, the assertion that keystones "improve health and robustness" is a bit of an anthropomorphic stretch that conveniently fits the mental model they are working with. And most importantly, they miss the ecos- in ecosystems (Okey 2004). Ecos- is derived from the Greek word Oikos, which means house or environment. Ecology is the study of the house, and relatedly, economics is the management of the house. In ecological terms, this includes both the abiotic (non-living things like rocks, weather, climate, minerals, etc.) and biotic (living things like trees, animals, soil microbes, lichen, etc.) factors that influence ecosystem function. So, when the term business ecosystem is used as an elaborate metaphor to describe the interactions of companies (i.e., biotic factors, organisms or living things), it completely misses the rest of the *Ecos* metaphor—the abiotic factors. These organisms are in a constant dialog of information seeking and feedback with these abiotic factors. To miss this in the framing of business ecosystem is to overlook half of the entire biological story. This is no small oversight. And yet, it has rarely been addressed by those with business acumen. So, while it is exciting to find so many researchers and practitioners learning from natural models, it is concurrently disappointing when these metaphors get misused and abused.

In an effort to better equip you with a baseline understanding of ecology, let us review a few fundamental concepts that are crucial to the study of ecosystems. While this is not intended to be a complete review, it is an introduction to the basic ideas that guide ecological thinking. We will discuss some basic ecological concepts such as energy and nutrient flows, food webs, succession, and the feedback loops that lead to self-regulation.

Despite their seemingly still and docile appearance, ecosystems represent a complex network of dynamic interactions. These interactions create an elaborate system of exchange that results in a dynamic equilibrium. There is a balance of sorts, but that balance is always changing and adjusting to the combination of abiotic and biotic factors that surround it. A good way to visualize the biosphere in dynamic equilibrium is to imagine a ball inside of a bowl. The bowl is representative of the abiotic (remember, that is non-living) factors in the biosphere. The ball is representative of all of the biotic (or living) factors on earth. As the conditions on earth are always shifting and changing (e.g., the tides coming and going, wind patterns moving air, rivers moving sediments, and most recently, drastically changing climates), envision the bowl always moving and shifting from side to side, tilting back and forth. In response, the ball (i.e., Life) is always rolling from one side of the bowl to another, always adjusting itself to find the place of the least amount of momentum, where it requires the least amount of energy to hold position. In living systems, dynamic equilibrium refers to the ball's constant reorientation to stay in the lowest place in the bowl.

In order to do this, Life leverages the interdependent relationships with other organisms and species to form elaborate patterns of water, energy, and nutrient cycling. A part of the process of adapting to these changing conditions is the exchange of materials and energy that results in the whole system remaining in dynamic equilibrium. This exchange of abiotic factors among living communities results in the seemingly stable systems that we can see as we sit on the bank of stream or rest on a forest hike.

The next ecological concept worth mentioning is succession. Succession refers to the developmental phases that an ecosystem goes through over time in which it matures from one biological community to another. I will use the example of the five acres I grew up on in rural Illinois to exemplify how succession happens.

My parents have lived on this piece of land for nearly 45 years, and in that time, the land use and the ecological patterns of the landscape have changed quite substantially. Their property is on a distinct biogeographical area referred to as the Driftless Area notable for its deep valleys and high bluffs. It has the rich topsoil characteristic of the Midwest of the United States and the ecosystem is dominated by oaks and a few other species of hardwoods. Their lot is composed of a steep hillside that levels into a flood plain and a creek that joins the Mississippi River about two miles downstream. While the wooded hillside has remained relatively stable over the last 45 years, with only the intermittent falling tree, the bottomlands have been incredibly dynamic and resilient.

Throughout my childhood, the bottom was dominated by grasses and annual plants that would frequently tower over my curious head. There were very few trees, except by the banks of the creek. Our neighbors' steady population of grazing cows and horses maintained this ecosystem, preventing the possibility that young trees could take hold. Biodiversity was relatively low, and interdependence was less consequential for the organisms involved. Nevertheless, these annual plant and grass species were modifying the soil conditions, building up a dense base of absorbent biomass in the soil, enabling it to slow rain and cycle nutrients with impeccable effectiveness. This grassy era represents one distinct successional phase in this system.

Then, sometime in my late childhood and early teens, the horse-loving neighbors moved away and the farm upstream changed hands, leaving the grassland on its own and providing enough stability that hardier woody shrubs and trees had a chance to establish themselves. The first trees to move in were mulberry and elder, both quick growing, soft wood tree species that are tolerant of the high water table. Leveraging the stability and physical conditions created by the previous successionary species, these trees also cycle through nutrients in their life spans. However, they create even greater stability in the system by taking several years to assimilate water, nutrients, and energy, and then, at the end of their life cycle, those nutrients are then broken down more slowly than the grasses and annual plants. The multi-tiered structure of a woodland invites a diversity of bird and mammal species that did not have sufficient shelter in a grassland and species settle into ever more complex niches. This softwood forest represents a second successional phase.

These successionary phases have been intermittently disturbed by flash flooding that redistributes nutrients from the muddy creek bed, further diversifying the chemical and biological composition of the flood plain soils. Disturbance is also a key component of succession because it enables new species to move into an otherwise stable system.

At present, my parents are maintaining this softwood forest in a park-like environment and promoting the next successional phase by mowing all but some patches of wild berries and flagging all of the young oak trees that have started popping up. They hope to bring it back into an oak savannah-like ecosystem through time, and so far, they are well on their way to shepherding in this next successional phase.

Succession is a valuable concept for many different contexts of change, growth, and development—for a landscape, for an organization, and as I am writing, its suddenly obvious to me that this change is also reflective of my parents' lives and the phases of the family that they have created together. Through time, succession leads to greater levels of stability and higher levels of interdependence among organisms, with various niches developing intricate relationships with one another. That tiny floodplain in the midst of the Driftless Area—with all of its bold rocky cliffs and flood-tolerant lifestyles—provides a model for resilience through time and the varied rhythms of Life.

A few other ecological concepts are scattered throughout the rest of this text, and there are many more levels of detail to be explored, if you should feel so inclined. This overview is intended to give you a basic level of vocabulary to talk, think, and strategize with ecological literacy.

To close out this chapter, let us reiterate that biologically inspired management innovations for most organizations tend to be inwardly focused and help managers to reconceive how they think about their organizations. Traditionally, we have viewed management as a hierarchical, top-down approach to getting things done that emphasizes the leadership driving the company's agenda and employees enacting that agenda. Biologically inspired management innovations provoke new models of getting work done that de-emphasize these hierarchies and attempt to emulate the organizational principles of Life sometimes referring to swarms or complex adaptive systems. For some organizations, these innovations do little to change the way that an organization interacts with socioecological systems, and consequently, have little to do with sustainability outside of the organizational boundaries. These management innovations are typically influential for organizational structures and interactions, and they tend to emphasize the act of managing and not necessarily the act of managing in a complex, dynamic context. To the contrary, other organizations combine the concept of being like nature with their desire to have a net positive impact on socioecological systems. These goals drive their emulation of biological principles. These organizations are a rare breed, indeed. These organizations are aiming to *be sustainable like nature*, the highest of sustainability aspirations.

CHAPTER 4

Innovations in Operations

Following on from the largely metaphorical uses of bioinspiration applied in management innovations, let us now dive into the more analogous uses of biological inspiration that provide tangible benefits for the material aspects of the business. This chapter gives a summary of several operational approaches and strategies inspired by nature, including industrial ecology, and models for the place-based management of facilities.

Industrial Ecology: An Idea With Generational Metamorphosis

To take a step into my research wormhole for a moment, the primary objective of a PhD research project is to *make an original contribution to knowledge*, and yet, the further I got into the process, the more I wondered if there was ever a new idea in the universe. They all seem to be a metamorphosed version of a proceeding idea, making it difficult to discern a butterfly from a caterpillar. While it is beyond the scope of this book to delve into a detailed analysis of the history of biological inspiration for innovation and industry, it is helpful to understand why some concepts seem so similar yet have different names and followings. In short, it is because they are very similar. The links between bioinspiration and industrial ecology are innumerable, and the differences are primarily related to scale of use and the disciplines of users. This section provides an overview of the discipline of industrial ecology, which is an older, and perhaps, more technically inclined, sibling of biomimicry that has its own academic programs, scholarly journals, and annual conferences.

The first rumblings of this idea date back to the 1940s, but the concept was solidified in a 1989 issue of *Scientific American* (Frosch and Gallopoulos 1989). Frosch and Gallopoulos posed these questions:

Why would not our industrial system behave like an ecosystem, where the wastes of a species may be resource to another species? Why would not the outputs of an industry be the inputs of another, thus reducing use of raw materials, pollution, and saving on waste treatment?

These provocations have led to a number of practices, many of which you may be familiar with today.

Let us pause here for a moment and address some basic principles of ecology. As discussed earlier, ecology is the study of interactions among organisms, different species, and their environment.

Broadly speaking, industrial ecology is concerned with an overall shift from a take–make–waste economic model to closed-loop, interconnected manufacturing and waste management model. As in biological systems where there is no such things as waste, industrial ecology models strive for zero waste as well. At this stage in its development as a discipline, it includes numerous specialized tools and processes, many of which are focused on modeling the nutrient (i.e., resource) flows through an industrial or product life cycle. This detailed quantification has enabled extensive analysis and data to inform product design and manufacturing decision making. Two specific approaches will be addressed in more detail: Life cycle analysis and industrial symbiosis.

Life Cycle Analysis and Planning

Most corporations perform some level of life cycle analysis (LCA) and planning as part of their overall environmental and social responsibility agenda, so this section will be brief to avoid belaboring the issue too much. LCA is an assessment of a product's material, energy, and in some cases, social impacts throughout the product's existence. It includes the impacts associated with extraction of raw materials, manufacturing, distribution to consumers, use by consumers, repair and maintenance, and where the product ends up after its first intended useful life span.

Let us consider an example: the infamous disposable plastic cup. The life cycle of a plastic cup can be broken down into several phases, and each phase can be described in terms of tons of carbon dioxide emitted, gallons of fresh water required, kilowatts of energy used, parts per million of toxic substances A, B, and C created, amount of habitat disturbed, and other metrics. So, without going into the exact numbers, let us just consider the life cycle.

These cups are typically made from virgin plastic, which requires petroleum. The extraction of petroleum can be a dangerous job for those involved and frequently requires time away from family and social infrastructure. Petroleum production also requires the use of land and energy and typically has negative impacts for biodiversity due to habitat destruction and noise, air, and water pollution. As we all know, crude oil is highly toxic, carcinogenic, and suspect in a number of birth defects and other ailments. The crude oil is then heated until it separates into constituent parts (gas, paraffin, diesel, etc.) using more energy. The separated oil-based materials are then delivered to another factory where more water and energy is used to process the crude oil into tiny bits of No. 6 thermoplastic polystyrene. From there, the tiny bits of No. 6 are shipped to the factory that makes the cups. They are melted down, color added, and then poured into molds—this facility also requiring energy, water, and causing other emissions. The shipping to distributors and the distribution process via storefront sales to consumers uses energy, water, and materials. If we wanted to get really detailed, we can consider who drives where to pick up the cups to be used by the consumer. Are they delivered or shipped via online purchase? And, alas, they arrive at the consumer where they are used for 15 min to a few hours. We have then reached the first *end of life*. From here, they can be washed and reused, recycled, or thrown away. You are probably getting the point that each of these options also has water, energy, and biodiversity implications. Number 6 plastics are infamously difficult to recycle because most municipalities can only manage a few other plastic numbers, No.1s and 2s being the most common. Not to mention that No.6s are often times combined with other materials. Disposable razors, for example, are difficult to separate out the metals from the plastics. And contrary to Toby Keith's tributary song about Red Solo Cups they are not decomposable in 14 years. No.6s require something more like 50 years to begin to decompose, left alone in the landfill.

Phew, deep breathe. That was a whirlwind tour of the life span of a single common object that we frequently interact with. And it is only made of one material! Now use that same lens for your television or your car, which are made of hundreds of different materials. This suddenly gets very complex, indeed. But this is the essence of LCA: look at every single phase of a product's life and determine the ways that it interacts with socioecological systems. The completion of an LCA and subsequent planning resulting from this information has been tremendously helpful for businesses to understand their impacts and the opportunities to reduce their impacts. It is a very effective approach that encourages incremental innovations and efficiencies and has been broadly applied across sectors.

Following from the new insights revealed with LCAs, extended producer responsibility also became popular in the 1990s through today as a way to build the cost of disposal into the cost of the product as the consumer pays for it. With that additional money, infrastructure is developed to recycle, remanufacture, or safely dispose of materials that are difficult for municipal waste departments to manage. This strategy pushes the responsibility of dealing with the entire life cycle of the product back to the producer, further incentivizing recycling, design for disassembly, and closed-loop manufacturing (discussed more later). This is an especially useful strategy for items that are especially ubiquitous, difficult to dispose of, or hazardous such as packaging, tires, car batteries, and electronics.

To further the industrial ecology perspective, if we put the LCA of one product into the context of several other products, we can then begin to see the relationships among manufacturing processes. For some companies, the LCA has also helped them to view their relationships with other members of their supply chain differently as well. These interactions can be leveraged for greater efficiency and integration of manufacturing processes across different sectors, potentially closing the loop for some resources or reusing energy and heat for more than one process, a practice known as industrial symbiosis.

Industrial Symbiosis

Following from an expanded ecological metaphor, some companies are considering themselves part of an industrial ecosystem of producers and consumers. These companies, frequently located in close proximity, share resources such as information, materials, and energy in an effort to improve overall sustainability for all participants. The companies involved in industrial symbioses range from pharmaceutical companies, agricultural product manufacturers, energy producers, and municipalities. Two examples are provided to demonstrate the variety of possibilities.

Kalundborg, Denmark, is home to the most famous example of an eco-industrial park that is now more than 25 years in operation. Although it was not originally designed for industrial symbiosis, today it includes over 30 material and energy exchanges among its nine industrial partners, a few of which are highlighted here for demonstration. The founding energy company provides residual steam to an oil refinery in exchange for gas to make more power. A local fish farm also receives steam from this plant, as do 3,500 homes equipped with steam heating systems. Additionally, the power company produces fly ash that is used by a cement company and waste gypsum goes to a company that produces gypsum board. Another company turns sulfur taken from the gas refining process into sulfuric acid. The fish farm sells sludge as fertilizer to nearby farmers, and water is reused by several different companies within the organization. Kalundborg was the first of its kind to demonstrate that co-location and resource sharing could result in competitive advantage, and today, it continues to be an international model for eco-industrial development.

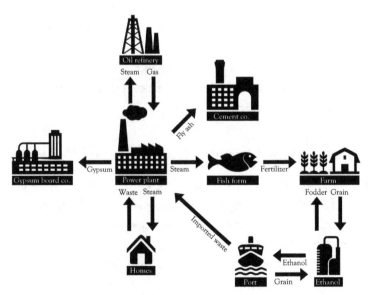

Figure 4.1 Industrial symbiosis at Kalundborg

Source: Author.

A second project, the Cardboard-to-Caviar project, is a small industrial ecosystem that emphasizes organic materials. It starts with waste cardboard boxes that are shredded and used as horse bedding in equestrian centers. The stables are cleaned and the soiled bedding is then fed to worms. When the worms have packed on enough pounds, they are then fed to sturgeon whose eggs will be sold as caviar. Simple, eh. This life cycle thinking takes what would otherwise be a waste product (i.e., cardboard) and by optimizing a series of biological processes, turns it into a high-value product.

At this point, you are probably trying to work out the difference between business ecosystems and industrial ecosystems, right? It is a mess of terms, really. But let me try to tease it apart for you. Business ecosystems are largely a metaphorical lens used to understand the relationships between different types of organizations. They try to explain supply chains as a network rather than a chain and use ecological roles to help companies define how they participate in these networks at a conceptual level. Industrial ecosystems, on the other hand, are more of an analogical construct, looking at the material and energy flows between companies in a tangible, physical way. While industrial ecosystems include places such as Kalundborg, they also include other kinds of resource sharing such as shared logistics coordination, green technology purchasing blocks, green building retrofits with several partners, and other types of projects.

Moving on to the next operational applications of bioinspiration, the following are more focused on how a single company views its own operations as a series of biological processes.

Place-Based Facility Management and Design

We will now take a slightly different angle on bioinspiration in operations and look at the design and management of facilities themselves, rather than the interaction of various facilities. There are several ways to incorporate bioinspiration into the design and management of facilities, and we will discuss two examples: (1) The Living Building Challenge and (2) Ecological Performance Standards.

The Living Building Challenge

The Living Building Challenge is a building certification (similar to LEED or BREEAM) created by the Living Futures Institute in 2006 that encompasses many principles of bioinspiration and regenerative design. This certification program starts with the premise that a building should, like a flower, give more to the world than it takes. Alleging to be the most rigorous performance standard for buildings in the world, the certification is based on a set of "Imperatives" for the design of a building, landscape, neighborhood, or community. These Imperatives (Table 4.1) are divided into seven categories and include:

Table 4.1 Living Building Challenge Imperatives

Category	Imperatives			
Site	Limits to growth	Urban agriculture	Habitat exchange	Human-powered living
Water	Net positive water			
Energy	Net positive energy			
Health	Civilized environment	Healthy interior environment		Biophilic environment
Materials	*No Red List*	Embodied carbon footprint	Responsible industry	Living economy sourcing	Net positive waste
Equity	Human scale + humane places	Universal access to nature and place	Equitable investment	*JUST* organizations
Beauty	Beauty + Spirit		Inspiration + Education	

Source: Adapted from The Living Future Institute 2017.

The Living Building Challenge has been achieved by a variety of private and public builders and remodelers. While many of the buildings have been in educational settings, some larger-scale commercial office projects have also been done. One example by a familiar name is the PNC Bank Davies and Andrew Branch in Fort Lauderdale, FL, that has met the Net Zero Energy Certification requirements, a stepping stone toward meeting the Living Building Challenge in its entirety. PNC Bank has significant experience building to LEED standards and used the Living

Building Challenge to surpass their existing performance goals. This and other case studies are available at the Living Future's website.

Ecological Performance Standards

Another bioinspired approach to facilities management is the application of Ecological Performance Standards. The concept was first described by Kevin Stack, a builder and the proprietor of Northeast Natural Homes who has training in biology and forestry. He began with the premise that the buildings that we put on any given piece of land should make the same contributions to the ecosystem that the original organisms would have done sans development. For instance, an oak forest is host to three layers of vegetation that each perform functions as they interact with rainfall such as slowing, filtration, and evapotranspiration (i.e., the release of water back into the air through the surface of leaves, similar to the steam that comes out in our breath). These functions occur at particular rates that vary by season and weather conditions.

So, if we take those three layers of vegetation out of the ecosystem in an area spanning 100,000 sq. ft. and put an office building in its place, we have suddenly lost the ecological functionality of water slowing, filtering, and evapotranspiration that are vital to our wellbeing and that of the other species that maintain the balance of the system. In fact, our tendency in water management is to do the opposite of slowing, filtering, and purifying in place. We typically move water away from our buildings as fast as possible and channel into ever-larger artificial waterways and canals that collect dirt and pollutants along the way and deposit them into our rivers and oceans.

Ecological Performance Standards, on the other hand, asks us to consider our buildings as part of that system of water management that slows, filters, and releases water on site and to the same level of water quality that the native ecosystem would. Our buildings can perform these functions any number of ways using technologies that already exist and innovative technologies yet to be developed to meet these performance criteria. For instance, we may utilize simple, common methods of water retention such as bioswales (shallow pools designed to capture and slow run-off from paved surfaces), multi-tiered landscaping to mimic the native system, or living plant walls to perform the same functions. As another example, we might utilize a green roof to perform some of these functions. But instead of using a design based on aesthetics or low maintenance needs, we design the green roof to meet the performance criteria for evapotranspiration that the native system would, influencing the larger climactic patterns of the region.

This example is just water-related ecosystem functions. Consider similar performance standards for carbon cycling, phosphorous and nitrogen cycling, biodiversity levels, and other functions. We can (and in my humble opinion, should) develop Ecological Performance Standards for all ecosystem functions that we can.

Biomimicry 3.8 further developed this concept by applying it to the level of entire new cities built from the ground up, and incorporated it into redevelopment plans for other cities on at least four continents. At the level of the organization, Interface Carpets is also applying this approach to the redesign of their factories, beginning with a remodel near Atlanta, Georgia. Details on this case study were scant at the time of publication, as it was still at the early, experimental phases of development.

At this stage, the concept is steadily gaining traction, and our technologies are increasingly sophisticated and accessible to enable this sort of innovation. Smart building technologies and the Internet of Things continue to enable new ways to collect data and make that data meaningful for new applications. It is technologically feasible to enact Janine Benyus's vision that "Humans will be truly sustainable when our cities are functionally indistinguishable from our forests." It may seem a far stretch, but a few leaders are paving the way as we speak.

Conclusion

To sum up this chapter, we have taken a look at how bioinspiration is applied in a few ways to operations management, from a large-scale perspective. Industrial ecology and all of its accompanying tools provide insights into the ecological principles that can guide cooperation among organizations and how they can provide insights into the impacts of products. The Living Building Challenge and Ecological Performance Standards also provide alternative lenses into the management of facilities based on the principles and functions of nature.

The next chapter will dive into some of the practical tools available to apply bioinspiration to product and process design, emphasizing technological applications of biological inspiration.

CHAPTER 5

Innovations in Product Development

As mentioned early on, the uses of bioinspiration for product design are the examples most frequently cited in popular media. When I give intro presentations, product examples are always at the forefront because of their bite-sized, easy-to-digest stories with nice images that clearly show how an innovation is like a biological model. This goes a very long way to spark the imagination, so I will present this chapter in a similar spirit. We will start with engineering, then move into materials and green chemistry, and finally, talk about the broader approaches to product design.

Bioinspiration in Engineering

One of the most classic stories of bioinspiration comes from Japan, a very mountainous country with an efficient, high-speed rail system. And like any modern, mountainous transit, these high-speed trains pass through tunnels along their way. However, at some point, they began experiencing problems with the passage of these trains through tunnels because as they moved through the tunnels, they would build up a pressure gradient at the front of the train, and when they emerged from the other side, they would create a loud tunnel boom as the pressure changed again. If you are living nearby one of these tunnels, human or non-human, a regularly scheduled sonic boom in your neighborhood can pose quite a problem. So, the story goes that one of the engineers with JR West who was working on this problem, Eiji Nakatsu, also happened to a birder. He had been mulling over this problem for some time, and one day, as he attended his local birding club meeting, it occurred to him that kingfishers (and diving birds, in general) experience the same conditions as the trains they were going between environments of low pressure to high pressure to low pressure again in a relatively short time span. And yet, when the king-fisher dives into the water, it hardly makes a splash and surely does not produce a sonic boom. So, he got to thinking and eventually produced a model of the front of a train, which resembled that of the beak of a kingfisher—long and narrow and slightly pointed. And sure enough, the newfound hydro- and aerodynamicism also solved the problem for the high-speed trains, and the loud boom was no more to boot, this new shape also increased its speed by 10 percent and uses 15 percent less electricity than the previous design. A win all around. For more information about this case study and photos of the kingfisher and the train, do a quick search at AskNature.org.

This type of optimization inspired by nature is common among engineers and architects who are always looking for solutions to light-weighting, material optimization, and energy reduction strategies, which are bountiful among biological phenomena. An example of material optimization that has been prolific in the design world is that of trees. For the purposes of example, we will look specifically at the optimization of the Scots pine trees, which withstand a variety of windy and rough conditions, and are able to do so because of a strategy referred to as load-adaptive growth. This basically means that the tree responds to environmental pressures by growing more material where more strength is needed and not dedicating material and energy resources to those areas where it is not necessary. Envision a tree at the top of a windy hill that has dense, thick branches on one side and long, reaching branches on the other. At the more local scale, this is a product of the tree expending materials where they are most needed for the entire tree to remain standing on the one side and collect the greatest amount of solar radiation on the other side. The exact rate of this trade-off in terms of materials applied to the various joints has been calculated for various applications. A researcher named Claus Mattheck at the Karlsruhe Research Centre in Germany has developed a few programs to facilitate it in the form of CAO (computer-aided optimization) and SKO (soft kill option) software.

A biomimetic designer recently applied similar thinking to a water bottle redesign. The client was not necessarily looking for a biomimetic solution, but the designer, Carlos Rego from LogoPlaste Design certainly was. Having been a long-time practitioner of sustainable design practices and a recent graduate of Biomimicry 3.8's Biomimicry Specialist program, he was keen to get his hands dirty with some practical application of his new skills. The opportunity arose when Vitalis, a popular brand of bottled water in Portugal, was seeking to redesign their PET water bottles in response to a United Kingdom mandate to reduce the materials in plastic packaging. Carlos led a team at the LogoPlaste Innovation Lab through a search for new designs that could be lightweight and strong and first turned to AskNature.org (a search engine of nature's functions that we will explore more later). They toyed around with several potential bio-inspired solutions and the version that demonstrated the most promise in their modeling process was based on the spiraling growth patterns found in some pine trees, specifically the Scots pine. The Scots pine's branches are composed of helical fibers, and it twists its branches in response to repeated strong winds. The design team took this principle of helical structures and applied it to various angles and in different thicknesses and depths into the structure and curvature of the plastic. When analyzed using finite element analysis, they found that the resulting bottle reduced total raw material use by 7 percent, making it the lightest PET bottle on the market. This case study is well-documented on AskNature.org and includes photos of both the Scots pine and the Vitalis bottle.

There are many, many more examples, but this gives a taste of the methods, tools, and technologies for biomimetic design within the purview of engineering and structural applications. Next we will move on to the materiality of things, putting on the lenses of chemistry and material science.

Chemistry Done Nature's Way

Before we dive into examples of chemicals and materials that mimic nature, let us spend a moment looking at the bigger picture of how nature does chemistry, as this tends to be a bit of an intimidating topic for non-scientists. There is one particular subset of Life's Principles (from Biomimicry 3.8) that are particularly relevant to chemicals and materials: "Use Life-Friendly Chemistry." Let us spend a bit of time unpacking these principles to lay the foundation for a broader understanding beyond just a few biomimetic case studies. The premise of life-friendly chemistry is that organisms produce all chemicals and materials on or near their own bodies, making it critical that these materials do not interfere with their own ability to survive and thrive. Toxics are rarely used, and when they are deemed necessary (in the form of snake venom, for instance) they are produced in small quantities, on demand at the place of use, and they break down into benign particles after their useful life has been served—which typically lasts a short amount of time.

That leads us to the next Life's Principle related to this category "Break down products into benign constituents." Let us take an example of long-chain carbons, which are prolific in the modern world. "They are?," you may be asking. Indeed, long-chain carbons that we rely on today can be found in anything made from fossil fuels such as petroleum and coal. As we have discussed already, fossil fuels have a whole slew of associated issues, environmental persistence being one of the most troubling. Plastics, chemicals, and other polymers are infamously difficult to get rid of and build up in living tissues through a process called bioaccumulation, also sometimes referred to as biomagnification. Bioaccumulation occurs when tiny amounts of toxic, hormone-disrupting, or carcinogenic chemicals are absorbed by tiny plants and microscopic creatures at the bottom of the food web. These tiny critters are then consumed by larger critters, but as they are digested, the chemicals do not leave the bodies of the consumers and instead remain persistent in their tissues. And in turn, when these animals are consumed by those further up in a food web, even larger amounts are absorbed and persist. And so on, up to the top tiers of carnivores in any given system. In many cases, humans are the top-level carnivores, and these persistent chemicals end up in our bodies where they can wreak havoc. (This is the reason I stopped eating tuna over 10 years ago. If high concentrations of mercury—originating from coal fire power plants—are unsuitable for pregnant women and young children, they should not be suitable for anyone, in my humble opinion. But I digress!)

This ecology lesson is included not to depress you or make you a picky eater, but as a means of comparison. If we compare these fossil fuel-based chemical processes to those found in natural systems, we find that nature's chemistries are also producing long-chain carbons as building blocks for materials. In fact, several plants such as the rubber and pine trees, camelina, tobacco, and oil-producing varieties have all been investigated as potential alternative sources of hydrocarbons. These plant-based materials can be used for numerous fuels and plastic products, some of which we are starting to see in biodegradable tableware, for instance. It is only logical that we need single-use forks to have a lifespan reflective of this single use, designed to break down at the end of their intended useful life. That is what nature does. It only puts the chemical durability into its materials to last for the entirety of its intended use. And beyond that, it welcomes the next microbial user to have at it. The major difference is that nature's materials break down into components that are digestible by microbes, fungus, and plants, and they can be harmlessly assimilated into the creation of new materials without persistent toxicity. This is the essence of breaking down into benign constituents—no unwanted by-product particles left behind.

One product example demonstrating these two principles is called PureBond®, an adhesive used in laminated wood products produced by Columbia Forest Products. There is a problem in the built environment frequently referred to as *sick building syndrome*. It can have many different causes, but in new buildings, it is usually caused by the off-gassing of new building materials that contain volatile organic compounds (VOCs), such as formaldehyde. It is estimated that over half of all formaldehyde made each year is used in wood adhesives (Lin et al. 2007).

As an academic researcher in Wood Science and Engineering, Dr. Kaichang Li was familiar with the challenges of adhesives building materials. It was during an evening of coastal mussel harvesting, Dr. Li was struck by the ability of the mussels to cling to the rocks in such rough and rapidly changing condition. As he dug into the literature on blue mussel adhesives, he uncovered a large body of research investigating the chemical properties of their byssus threads that enabled them to stick to a variety of surfaces including Teflon, steel, and glass (Lin et al. 2007). He toyed around with a few ideas to emulate this adhesive and landed on a modified soy protein adhesive as a potential solution. He then found industrial development partnerships with two companies in the forestry industry—Hercules and Columbia Forest Products—and through a series of joint proprietary funding, development, and IP arrangements with these two companies and Oregon State University (where Dr. Li was on faculty) created the now commercially lucrative product, PureBond. In 2007, they won the Presidential Green Chemistry Challenge Award, and by 2010, over 40 million PureBond panels had been manufactured and sold. It has been a major success for biomimetic innovation.

The next of the Life's Principles related to chemistry is to "Build selectively with a small subset of elements." Despite the enormity of the periodic table, most living organisms are composed of just six very common elements: carbon, hydrogen, oxygen, nitrogen, phosphorous, and sulfur (see Table 5.1). Many other elements, varying by kingdom and by species, such as silica, calcium, magnesium, zinc, and others, are also common in living systems, though they are found in trace amounts. In short, Life utilizes a few common components that are plentiful and easy to access and assimilates them into a variety of more complex molecules. Common things are valuable for biological organisms. This is in comparison to humans who tend to place high value on rare things (think gold, platinum, silver, etc.) and low value on common things (water, forests, labor) until they become rare.

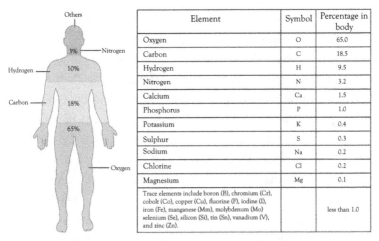

Element	Symbol	Percentage in body
Oxygen	O	65.0
Carbon	C	18.5
Hydrogen	H	9.5
Nitrogen	N	3.2
Calcium	Ca	1.5
Phosphorus	P	1.0
Potassium	K	0.4
Sulphur	S	0.3
Sodium	Na	0.2
Chlorine	Cl	0.2
Magnesium	Mg	0.1
Trace elements include boron (B), chromium (Cr), cobolt (Co), copper (Cu), fluorine (F), iodine (I), iron (Fe), manganese (Mm), molybdenum (Mo) selenium (Se), silicon (Si), tin (Sn), vanadium (V), and zinc (Zn).		less than 1.0

Table 5.1 The atomic composition of the human body

Source: Adapted from https://boundless.com/biology/textbooks/boundless-biology-textbook/the-chemical-foundation-of-life-2/atoms-isotopes-ions-and-molecules-50/the-periodic-table-275-11408/

To explore one technological example of this principle, we could view our over-abundance of atmospheric carbon as an opportunity, rather than a pollutant in our policies and technological interventions. This is exactly what Novomer is doing in its development of molecules that convert waste carbon dioxide into polymers. Its website specifies:

> Novomer's synthetic chemical technology allows traditional chemical feedstocks to be combined with carbon dioxide or carbon monoxide to cost effectively synthesize sustainable chemicals and materials for a wide variety of applications. The chemicals and materials contain up to 50% by weight low cost waste carbon dioxide (CO_2) or carbon monoxide (CO) and, as a result, have a significantly reduced carbon and energy footprint and advantaged economics as compared to the materials they will replace. Not only do the materials and chemicals offset the use of petroleum derived feedstocks, they also sequester the CO_2 and CO for the life of the product, mitigating global warming and climate change.
>
> *Source*: http://novomer.com/our-company

Sounds pretty promising, eh? Imagine what this could mean for the plastics industry. This could be a truly disruptive approach to the production of many common polymers such as those used in "diapers, paints, coatings, high performance plastics, and textiles." Diapers that sequester carbon!? This is revolutionary!

The final Life's Principle related to chemical processes is that Life does chemistry in water. Seems simple enough, right? How else does one do chemistry?, To date, the majority of modern industrial chemical interactions have been done in organic (i.e., petrochemical) solvents under high heat and pressures. And unfortunately, most chemistry degree programs do not require a course in toxicology, so many of the long-term impacts of chemical development and manufacturing are overlooked until they start to make people sick. Life, on the other hand, uses just one simple, versatile solvent—water. And it does so in or nearby a living organism. Consider an abalone shell, one of the toughest materials on earth (toughness being a material property related to its ability to resist cracking). This is done without chemical processing, high temperatures, or intense pressures to force it into shape and create its strength, as is required for human-made tough ceramics such as Kevlar and others. Abalone shells are made on the body of the abalone's muscle through the secretion of a protein template that collects calcium and carbon molecules from seawater. These molecules are then assembled into a more complex structure, calcium carbonate.

Let us now look at a product example with a similar strategy. (Calera and a few other similar companies) has developed a process to create calcium carbonate, which is a necessary component of the CO_2 behemoth concrete, in such a way that it results in a net sequestration of carbon. The way that they are doing this is somewhat similar to the abalone, through a process of mineralization via aqueous precipitation. With the co-location of their production facilities next to coal-fired power plants and to the sea, they are able to pump the flue gases through seawater and capture the CO_2 and other particles from the flue gases into a solid form that precipitates out of the solution. While the traditional cement requires the heating of mined limestone to a temperature of 2,640°F, releasing CO_2 every step of the way, Calera estimates that it sequesters a ton of CO_2 for every two tons of cement produced. In summary, four principles make up the guidelines for bioinspired chemistry:

Four Principles of Bioinspired Chemistry
- Use life-friendly chemistry
- Break down into benign constituents
- Build selectively with a small subset of elements
- Do chemistry in water

Now that we have laid the groundwork, let us demonstrate with a few case studies. In addition to numerous academic research settings, there are a few chemistry labs that are experimenting with bioinspired chemistry in partnership with private companies. The Warner Babcock Institute for Green Chemistry, located in Massachusetts, is a research lab that works in challenge-based partnerships with various industries, ranging from hair care to asphalt to develop new chemical formulations for their products. Similarly, Blue Marble Biomaterials in Missoula, Montana, is approaching the food industry with a new lens, and using a bioinspired approach to food colorings, artificial flavors, and other challenges in the clean food movement. Both of these companies work closely with bioinspiration consultants as part of their innovation processes.

In summary, the chemistry of Life has much to teach us about how to produce substances in ways that also support our own wellbeing. Although this section provides several examples, it really only scratches the surface on the field of biomimetic chemistry. Hopefully, it has provided some insights into the realm of possibilities for nature-inspired chemistry and what it might have to offer your industry.

Bioinspiration and Additive Manufacturing

One emerging approach to manufacturing that has generated a great deal of excitement is the 3D printer, also known as additive manufacturing. Following from the principle of using simple, common building blocks, additive manufacturing has piqued the imaginations of biomimics who see great potential in the rapid prototyping abilities of these machines and the versatility of their material feedstocks. Again, in this realm, it is important to maintain a critical sustainability lens, as some of the early feedstocks of additive manufacturing have demonstrated toxicity, but there are some promising projects emerging in this space. In fact, some of the earliest research using 3D printers has been in the area of green and biomimetic chemistries.

Given the novelty and explosive popularity of additive manufacturing in recent years, it is feasible that the 3D printer could become as ubiquitous as the personal computer has become in households, schools, workplaces, and maker labs. With this expansion comes the critical questions about the life cycle of these materials and outputs. Numerous groups, while broadly celebrating the democratization of manufacturing enabled by 3D printing, have been investigating the implications of localized production and consumption. What if every household was making their own jewelry, dishes, plastic bottles, and even hand guns? What are the implications of the materials used, and how do they fit into our material and waste management systems?

Autodesk, a maker of software applications and long-time proponent of bioinspiration (one of the original funders of AskNature.org), has been initiating some probing investigations into these questions.

As the potential creators of software for both commercial and domestic additive manufacturing, they are taking the lead on the "pursuit of more sustainable additive manufacturing and a better 3D printing user experience" (Floyd and Gladwin 2015). In 2015, Autodesk supported a group of researchers at the University of California Berkeley Center for Green Chemistry to explore the interface of green chemistry, bioinspiration, and 3D printing. This group identified eleven guidelines for biomimetic printing materials, similar to Life's Principles, but specifically written as guidelines for bioinspired additive manufacturing.

Guidelines for Bioinspired Additive Manufacturing
- Unity within diversity: Minimum part for maximum diversity
- Multi-tasking monomers: Relationships matter
- The optimal activator: The environment is the catalyst
- Taking advantage of gradients: Making delta do work
- Shape is strength
- Self-organization
- Bottom-up construction
- Hierarchy across linear scales
- Functionally graded material
- Composite construction
- Water is the universal medium

Source: McKeag (2015).

While these guidelines are specifically applied to additive manufacturing, they could be seen as more broadly applicable to other kinds of chemical manufacturing as well. The following examples provide a look into some emerging applications.

We will start with a glance into bioinspiration and additive manufacturing in the medical world. One common problem with tissue transplants is the rejection by the patient's body's natural defenses. In an effort to circumvent this problem, scientists in the health-care sector are exploring the 3D printing of tissue scaffolds customized to the specific needs and location of the patient's injury. Rather than trying to implant new tissues, this technology would create the structures that would promote the growth of the patient's own tissues, using the scaffold as a template of where to grow.

Another example is the use of additive manufacturing to mimic the structure of particular organisms and transfer their design to other applications. Researchers at the University of California—Riverside, for instance, have been analyzing the very tough material properties found on the appendage of the mantis shrimp. When hunting, the mantis shrimp flings its club-like appendage with such a force that it forms a cavitation bubble on the surface of its prey, causing it to crack open for a ready-made meal. The surface of this appendage is the location of a unique herringbone pattern that is of interest to researchers looking for novel structural and material properties. Using 3D printers for rapid duplication and then prototyping of the same pattern at a larger scale, they have been able to test this pattern with other materials and demonstrate how the pattern is able to distribute stress across the surface, reducing structural failure. They are interested in applying these learnings to several sectors such as automobiles, aerospace, safety equipment, and architecture.

These types of functional and material insights, coupled with the biomimetic principles for additive manufacturing and a big dose of sustainability thinking, could revolutionize the way we produce and consume products. If the prophecies are right, it could lead to some level of the democratization of manufacturing—both an exciting prospect and an enormous responsibility. Time will tell where this leads us, but the foundations of a sustainable path are already becoming clear.

Designing for Closed Loops

As mentioned before, one of the most important ecological principles for design, manufacturing, and waste management is the concept of *waste = food*. In short, this means that there is no such thing as waste in natural systems because every used material is a raw material for something else. There is no concept of throwing something *away* because *away* simply does not apply in a biophysical sense. All organisms are adept at taking advantage of the plentiful raw materials around them and using them for their own needs. In fact, some organisms evolve to take advantage of plentiful materials that no other organisms are interested in. Scientists have recently discovered microbes that eat plastic and nuclear waste, a task we thought impossible just decades ago. So, if we start to view all of our materials and waste with this lens, it is not a huge stretch to consider manufacturing in such a way that material loops are easily closed. There are a few ways in which this gets implemented, and it goes by slightly different names such as closed-loop manufacturing, design for disassembly, cradle-to-cradle, product leasing models, and related strategies in which a product is designed with its entire life cycle in mind.

> **Closed-Loop Design and Manufacturing:** An approach to design and business model innovation which emphasizes the bioinspired principle of *Waste = Food* and eliminates the concept of waste by creating circular product life cycles by design.

The best way to demonstrate closed-loop manufacturing is through an example, so we will take a close look at the design and life cycle of a carpet tile. As part of their overall mission to *be like nature*, Interface began innovating new ways to keep their products out of the landfill. Early on in this journey, they invited Dayna Baumeister, business partner of Janine Benyus, down to their offices near Atlanta, GA, for a workshop. The team—including designers, engineers, business associates, marketing, and some members of the leadership—took a walk out into the forest to ask the question "How does nature cover the floor?" As they toured around, they began to notice that there was an emergent pattern among the leaves, sticks, pinecones, and branches strewn about on the forest floor. The relative consistency of their chaotic arrangement produced an entropic pattern (i.e., one lacking order or predictability). If one piece of the forest floor was removed or relocated, it was nearly impossible to tell that it had been misplaced. They then went back into the studio and began developing new carpet tile designs based on this principle. The end result is a carpet tile line called Entropy™, which has since come to represent over 40 percent of their total sales. This carpet line is unique because the weave of the color of the fibers is somewhat random and a mix of various colors on an overall palette. This feature allows the tiles to be easily exchanged when they are worn without a noticeable difference in color, and it eliminates the need for the buyer to store extra carpet tiles to ensure that dye lots are the same, reducing waste on that end as well. This bioinspired redesign has been a major component of Interface's overall sustainability strategy.

A second aspect of Interface's closed-loop manufacturing strategy, which they refer to as ReEntry, was the invention of a carpet recycling machine called Cool Blue. Cool Blue's primary job is to remove carpet fiber from the nylon backing so that the nylon and fibers can be separated and sorted for recycling. Interface uses the nylon and sends the fibers back to their suppliers to be recycled into usable material for them. According to their website, they have reclaimed over 309 million pounds of carpet since 1995, but they also point out that an estimated 4.5 billion pounds are sent to the landfill in North America each year! That is an incredible amount of waste that is technologically accessible for recycling. Interface is forever on the lookout for cost-effective ways to incorporate used carpets back into their supply chain, and they currently do not have enough feedstocks to keep up with their production of new carpet tiles. One way that they are hoping to recirculate carpets more efficiently is through the development of legislation in several states that would make it illegal for carpets to be thrown into the landfill and push the responsibility of diversion back to the industry where they can drive recycling measures. As is evident in this example, just a few small changes in design and equipment can drive enormous changes throughout an entire industry.

Design for disassembly, which is related to closed-loop manufacturing, refers to the front-end of a product's life in which decisions are made about how a product is designed and held together so that they can be easily taken apart at the end of their useful life. A few basic principles apply such as use as few parts as possible, so there is less to take apart, the fewer fasteners the better, use simple, common fasteners, avoid glues whenever possible, and include instructions, so the user knows how to disassemble and recycle the product at the end of its life span.

Again, we will refer to an example from Interface. Designers and engineers at Interface were well aware that one of the major impacts of their product was the glue that was used to hold the carpet tiles down. Throughout its entire life cycle, the glues caused problems, ranging from off-gassing toxicity to the difficult removal of tiles when they need to be replaced. In search of another solution, they began to ask the question

"How does nature hold down the forest floor?" and quickly came to the realization that gravity is the strongest force at play. They then began to brainstorm ways in which they, too, could leverage gravity to hold carpet tiles down. They soon devised a solution now known as Tactiles™, which are small adhesive squares that are attached to the carpet tiles where the four corners come together on the floor. Simply by attaching these corners, the collective weight of the overall carpet holds each individual square in place. Without the sticky backing and consequent destruction of glued tiles caused during removal, the tiles are recyclable via the ReEntry® program.

The Cradle-to-Cradle™ design certification is based largely on the principles of design for disassembly, but also contains other specifications in five categories: material health, material reutilization, renewable energy and carbon management, water stewardship, and social fairness. It is considered one of the most stringent product certifications, on par with the Living Building Challenge in its respective category. McDonough and Braungart, the founders of this certification program, began with a book of the same name in which they describe the nature-based principles of a Cradle-to-Cradle™ process. One of the most popular concepts from this book is their advocacy that we stop thinking about products in terms of *eco-efficiency* and start thinking about *eco-effectiveness*. Eco-efficiency, they argue is merely doing less bad and simply killing the planet at a slower pace. Eco-effectiveness, on the other hand, promotes a closed-loop manufacturing process that includes both technical and organic nutrient loops and a system of production and consumption that eliminates the concept of waste. At the time of writing, there were nearly 500 certified products on their website and undoubtedly more in development.

Product leasing models, also referred to as product servitization, is another approach to closed-loop manufacturing. One example of this is a partnership between Phillips and Turntoo—or more specifically, with the architect founder of Turntoo, Thomas Rau. Rau was outfitting his office in Amsterdam with lighting and approached Phillips with a new model in which he would just pay per unit of light or lux. He did not care how he got that light, so he left it up to Phillips to figure out how to make it happen with a servitized model of lighting. Rau leaves the installation, management, replacement, and disposal of the light fixtures to Phillips and just pays them a service fee for taking care of it all. Given the success of this approach for his firm, Rau then went on to create Turntoo, a company that facilitates servitization of other products by managing the relationship between supplier, manufacturer, and end user. This type of model is becoming increasingly common in business-to-business sectors such as health care and starting to emerge in business-to-consumer markets.

Regenerative Innovation

One last concept related to new product development that is becoming increasing popular is something that I describe as *Regenerative Innovation*. This practice emerged as a pattern in my case study research, and after I started to notice it, I began to see it in a diversity of other companies as well. We will start with a few examples and then get into a specific definition.

To return to Interface yet again, as aforementioned, they were on the hunt for new sources of recycled material because their production of new carpets has been surpassing their ability to gather recyclable carpets. Consequently, they started looking for new sources of nylon to be recycled into carpet fibers, and they were concurrently interested in incorporating social equity as a factor of their innovation process. After some searching, they realized that one major source of waste nylon was in discarded fishing nets. Frequently, these nets are discarded in the oceans and on beaches once they develop holes and are no longer functional. Nets discarded in the oceans are a major source of pollution and are the culprit in *ghost fishing* where unintended fish, turtles, birds, and sea mammals get caught in abandon nets and die when they are unable to get out. In partnership with the London Zoological Society, Interface sought to create some financial and social infrastructure to collect discarded fishing nets and incorporate them back into their supply chain. They identified a pilot location in the Philippines where local fisherman and villagers are paid a modest wage for the collecting, cleaning, and bundling of discarded fishing nets that are then loaded into shipping containers and transported to one of Interface's suppliers in Eastern Europe where they are melted down in nylon fiber again. This pilot in the Philippines was such a success that Interface has developed it into a self-sustaining project called *Net-Works*, and they are currently expanding into Africa and exploring other locations.

Another example comes from Ecover, the domestic cleaning supply company. Among growing concerns about ocean plastic and the harm it is doing to our fisheries and coastlines, Ecover was inspired to do their part to raise awareness about this issue and also reincorporate ocean plastic back into their supply chain. In partnership with a Portuguese product design firm Logoplaste, which had a bit of a reputation for biomimetic product design, they developed a bottle made from recycled ocean plastic. The bottle was designed with structural inspiration from the radiolarian, a microscopic marine organism, to increase strength and reduce weight. Ecover also partnered with local fishermen and schools in the Netherlands to collect ocean and canal plastic and close the loop on their supply chain. At the end of the pilot project, the school children who gathered the plastic were given samples of the plastic bottles that they helped to create.

There are numerous other examples such as ocean plastic being used for skate boards and board shorts, and carbon sequestered from air pollution in China being converted into synthetic diamonds for jewelry. The list of case studies keeps growing every time I look. While it is similar to many other aspects of biomimetic design and innovation, it is unique from other described sourcing, recycling, and manufacturing methods in a few subtle ways. Rather than managing a waste stream that currently belongs to someone else, regenerative innovation creates infrastructure to utilize a pollutant and source of socioecological harm currently present in the global commons, creates novel value for the organization, and develops inclusive social capital while reducing ecological damage. The global commons part is key. The pollution that is being sequestered and upcycled does not belong to anyone or even a particular country. It is waste that is left to somebody else to clean-up. Like the detritus feeders of the soil, these companies are making something valuable out of waste the world has left behind and improving the wellbeing of people in the process.

> **Regenerative Innovation:** Innovation strategies that create infrastructure to utilize a pollutant and source of socioecological harm currently present in the global commons to create novel value for the organization and develop inclusive social capital while reducing ecological damage.

Conclusion

This chapter has introduced several bioinspired approaches to product design and innovation. It has reviewed closed-loop manufacturing approaches, design for disassembly, Cradle-to-Cradle certifications, servitization models, and finally, it has introduced a new concept, Regenerative Innovation. There are likely other variations on these themes, and now that you are developing a lens for viewing bioinspired innovations, you may discover others on your own.

The next chapter will take us out to the scale of the entire enterprise, beyond the reaches of the organization to take a look at the larger globalized economic system is inspired by nature's genius.

CHAPTER 6

Bioinspiration in the Global Context

The main objective of this chapter is to draw our perspective out to a global scale of interaction and identify some ecological stories and biomimetic approaches that can guide decision making in a global context.

When considering bioinspiration at a global scale, it can be helpful to take a holistic perspective. Although the term holistic is frequently associated with health care, holism also has a specific meaning in ecological terms. Ecological holism is the view that life self-organizes into layered whole systems—that is, the whole is greater than the sum of the parts. This creates an emergent environment where the same components can interact in different ways and create varied results. This conceptual framework is often also referred to as a complex adaptive system.

While this may seem like an abstract concept, it is also widely applicable to a global scale. Think of the Internet, social media, or the global economy. These are all systems nested in other systems that result in very complex behaviors when viewed as wholes. For the manager, this means that their organization is viewed in the larger socioeconomic and socioecological contexts. A firm grounding in this position is necessary to begin to apply bioinspiration at this larger scale of meaning. As discussed in Chapter 2 regarding the connections of bioinspiration to sustainability, no innovation can be viewed as sustainable in a larger context of unsustainability (Gaziulusoy 2015; Seebode, Jeanrenaud, and Bessant 2012). This chapter aims to help us identify how bioinspiration can help us to do this with a few approaches: resilience thinking, reconsidering competition and cooperation, and the circular economy.

Resilience True to the Biological Phenomena

Resilience has come to mean many things to many people in recent years. So many things, in fact, that it is difficult to discern if it actually means much of anything anymore. As we discussed in Chapter 2, resilience refers to the ability of a system to maintain functionality in the midst of a disturbance, and there are seven basic principles that guide the application of resilience according to the Stockholm Resilience Alliance (see text box below). We will spend a moment framing each principle for the perspective of a manager.

Principles of Resilience for Development
- Maintain diversity and redundancy
- Manage connectivity
- Manage slow variables and feedbacks
- Foster complex adaptive systems thinking
- Encourage learning
- Broaden participation
- Promote polycentric governance

Source: Simonsen et al. (2014).

It is now commonly accepted that diversity adds richness to our organizations, but we rarely reflect on the biological origins of trait. If we consider diversity at the ecosystem level, we see that diversity leads to greater levels of stability because of overall resistance to disturbance and a greater ability to recover from disturbance. This is because each specific species plays a particular role in an ecosystem and different niches are fulfilled, so a variety of functions are performed. For instance, when forests are in their most stable *conservation* phase of their life cycle, they contain a high diversity of species of plants and animals with tightly woven interactions. If you compare that to a less stable system, like a flood plain around a river, less stable systems tend to be dominated by a few plant species that quickly take up nutrients, stabilize soil, and create conditions conducive to greater diversity. Through time, this greater diversity means greater stability—until another disturbance comes along (see the following text for more info on complex adaptive systems).

At the same time that diversity leads to resilience, so does redundancy. In a management setting, redundancy has come to be known as a counterproductive and a waste of resources. However, in an ecosystem, having several species or organisms that perform the same function leads to greater resilience because, if one species is suddenly unable to perform that function, another organism can quickly take over and maintain the stability of the whole system. We tend to drive our organizations toward efficiency, but as we learn from natural systems, efficiency is only part of the picture. Efficiency must be balanced with the overall stability of the system—and sometimes, compromises must be made for the sake of redundancy.

Connectivity is also a crucial aspect of resilience, and obviously applicable in a globalized economy. In ecosystems, this takes many forms such as the underground network of fungus that connects trees within a forest. Once thought to be just another mushroom, these mycorrhizal fungi form elaborate communication networks among the roots of trees, passing nutrients and chemical signals around. When these networks are disrupted by a landslide or a bulldozer, the communication among the trees is also disrupted with effects on reproductive timing and other consequences. While it is important that these systems (and our business systems) maintain high levels of connectivity, it is also a vulnerability because, when this connectivity is disrupted, it can have catastrophic consequences for the entire system. Remember the last time your Internet connection was out for an entire work day? Absolute gridlock, right? Connectivity is important, and it must be managed for the highest possible level of resilience.

Feedback loops and slow variables also need to be managed. The human relationship with feedback is a very strange one at this moment in history. Throughout our evolution, we have gained increasingly astute observation skills that have enabled us to collect feedback from our environments with intricate detail. However, in recent decades, a few important things have happened. Through technology, improvements in shelter, and the consolidation of the agricultural sector, our ability to perceive the subtleties of our environments has been on the decline, simply because we do not rely on them as much as we used to. Concurrently, many of the environmental threats that are likely to harm us today are happening at a global scale, such as climate change and epidemics of disease. Up until now, we have not evolved to perceive feedback at a global scale, and it is a real vulnerability for us. Slow variables are also notoriously difficult to identify. Slow variables are those factors that change really gradually until all of the sudden—bam! —the entire system shifts because that one slow variable has changed so much. It is the little things that erode the structure, culture, and innovative capacity of an organization until one day, it suddenly finds itself in bankruptcy or a consumer relations crisis that it never recovers from many of the slow variables leading up to that crisis were likely present for a long time. Factors such as managerial cultures of competitiveness, maintenance of the status quo despite evidence of the need for change, and oblivion to shifting markets can all creep in slowly to our organizations, and before we know it, the company has to either fold or become completely different company. It is an interesting exercise to consider the slow variables in our workplaces, our health, and our relationships. What subtleties could suddenly become major vulnerabilities? Are we noticing the feedback from the systems around us?

The next attribute for resilience is to foster thinking in complex systems, as eluded to in the introduction to this chapter. For most of us, our training has taught us to break problems down into smaller parts so that we can understand precisely what the leverage point is to change the situation. However, this does not work for many kinds of problems. Many problems result from the complex interaction of several variables simultaneously and simply adjusting the volume of one variable or removing another variable will not solve the problem. It is rather that we need to influence several variables simultaneously to create adaptive behaviors of the overall system, adjusting the volume of multiple variables at the same time. Then we need to listen for feedback to see whether it worked and adjust again as needed. In summary, complex adaptive systems thinking embraces the complexity of everyday life and does not try to reduce it down to isolated variables. It is a way of viewing the world, not just a problem-solving approach.

Continuous learning and experimentation are also key components of resilient systems. These concepts are relatively common for most managers, so I will not go into detail, but I will say that these are also characteristics of other species as well. It is a bit oversimplified to say it this way, but our genes are learning in response to our environments and experiments (i.e., genetic mutations) are constantly occurring. It only makes sense that we should scale this up to our interactions with each other and our environments.

The last two principles promoted by resilience are also common for those attuned to socially responsible business practices. The first is to broaden participation in decision making to include a wider array of perspectives, build trust, and improve legitimacy of knowledge and authority through the decision-making process. The second is to utilize polycentric governance, which refers to the interaction of multiple governing bodies to create and enforce policies. This is pretty standard stakeholder engagement stuff, and less so in the realm of biological inspiration, but they present it as supportive of an overall resilience strategy, which some may find helpful.

As you can see here, there is a lot more to resilience than simply bouncing back after a disaster. Resilience is the integration of several factors and mindsets. The helpful aspect of understanding the biological underpinnings of resilience is that it enables us to seek the advice of other organisms along the way. Now that we have identified these principles, we can begin to ask "How do mangrove forests maintain resilience in a hurricane?"or "How do dandelions seem to be everywhere and always come back after we cut them down?" Each organism has its own strategies for resilience, and understanding some of the basic components of resilience can help us to identify those strategies.

Cooperation Versus Competition

Survival of the fittest. We have all heard it. Most of us have said it at one point or another. But where does that phrase actually come from? Most think that it comes from evolutionary theory, and it does—sort of. In Darwin's seminal work, "The Origin of Species," he does talk about fitness as an evolutionary advantage. As we know it today, we think about it as direct competition. The strongest survive. Kill or be killed. Many other hyper-aggressive interpretations that have been applied to a multitude of social systems, most obviously our economic system. However, this is not what Darwin said. This interpretation comes from a preeminent sociologist and influential thinker of the time, Herbert Spencer. What Darwin was saying had more to do with genes than it did with individuals. Fitness refers to the ability of one's offspring to survive so that the parents' genes are carried forward into successive generations. Fitness is only perceptible at the generational level, not at the individual level. Let us sit with that for a moment. We have 150 years of economic theory based on rational self-interest that if we make decisions based on our own personal success that it will equate to societal wellbeing. But if we are trying to stay true to the biology, we should be considering the interests of several generations down the line—and this is not a common practice.

As outlined in Table 6.1, the various kinds of relationships in natural systems have different consequences for each species involved. The first three—parasitism, predation, and herbivory—all have a positive effect for one species in the relationship and a negative effect for the other. To differentiate a bit, in parasitism, the parasite obtains food and shelter from the host, while predation is when a free-living organism catches and consumes another organism. Herbivory refers to one non-plant organism consuming a plant. It is a type of predation, but limited to cyclic interactions between plant and non-plant species.

Commensalism is when the interaction has a positive effect for one organism, but no effect for the other. A commonly cited example of this is the cattle egret and cattle. The cattle egret hangs around the cows because they stir up and attract insects as they walk and defecate, creating a feeding frenzy for the egrets. For the cow, it makes no difference if they are there or not (not in any way that we are of aware of, anyhow).

Table 6.1 Interactions among species

Species A	Species B	Name of interaction
+	−	Parasitism
+	−	Predation
+	−	Herbivory
+	0	Commensalism
+	+	Mutualism, Cooperation
0	0	Coexistence
−	−	Competition

Mutualisms or cooperative relationships are those interactions that have a positive outcome for both species involved. There many common examples of this, but one classic example is between bees, moths, and butterflies, and the flowers that they pollinate. These insects go from one flower to the next, collecting nectar to convert into sugars for their own purposes. However, in the process, they are also pollinating the flowers and enabling the plant's reproduction by carrying pollen from one flower to the next—a win-win strategy.

Coexistence is merely two organisms that share the same habitat, but manage to avoid competition and interaction for the most part because they occupy different ecological niches within the same habitat. There may be interactions among these species, but its inconsequential for both species. This might be two plants or animals that live in a tidal zone, for instance, but some live in the water and some live in the rocks. They eat different things and use different resources to create shelter for themselves. No big drama here.

The last interspecies relationship is the one we started with: competition. Think back to your earliest memories of the animal documentaries. You probably remember David Attenborough's cool voice giving the play-by-play of two rams butting heads, battling it out in competition for a mate, each of them trying to demonstrate dominance, or two monkeys fighting over fruit, high in the rainforest canopy. This competitive model was for a very long time, and often still today, seen as the major driving force of natural systems, where the toughest ram gets the girl and the quickest monkey gets the food.

However, enter sociobiologist E.O. Wilson in the late 1970s. His research on ants, bees, and other social species turned evolutionary theory on its head. This work gave rise to a whole new body of theory suggesting that cooperation is a much more common type of interaction than competition. At the time, this was a very unpopular idea. But today, most ecologists view natural systems in terms of interactions that mostly enhance one another with the occasional bouts of competition. While competition does happen, it is limited to brief interactions related to food and sex. And much more frequently, competition is avoided because it is a net energetic loss for both species. Avoidance of competition and niche differentiation are much more effective strategies for long-term survival.

Some researchers are even suggesting that altruism—that is, behaviors by an animal that benefit another species, but that may be detrimental to themselves—are also very common.

So if our economic models based on the very limited view of competition in which our innate need to compete for resources will eventually serve the common good are fundamentally flawed, where does that leave us? If cooperation, mutualistic, and coexisting behaviors actually dominate interactions in natural systems, what does that say about how we view commerce? Or rather, how we should view commerce?

Given that our survival as a social species is reliant upon our ability to cooperate, perhaps we need to be learning from the biological lessons of mutualisms like the mycorryhorizae and the complex interactive dynamics of the coral reef rather than competition? We have already seen how this can work in terms of materials with industrial ecology. If we zoom out to the level of the biosphere and global economy, this means that our economic interactions create value through balanced cooperative, mutualistic, and coexisting models that are embedded in socioecological systems. In the long run, its mutualisms that succeed.

Circular Economy

As mentioned early on, many of the concepts of bioinspiration have been repackaged several times for slightly different audiences. Once we start toying around with nature-inspired innovations, the possibilities are expansive and potential impact very broad. The circular economy concept epitomizes a tangible approach to bringing some of these big ideas into practice at the level of policy in systems of production and consumption. According to Wikipedia (which is arguably one of the most influential sources of information of our time), the circular economy framework is an umbrella term that includes systems thinking, biomimicry, industrial ecology, cradle-to-cradle, the Blue Economy, and The Biosphere Rules. As we have already covered four of these six subjects, we will only spend a moment on the last two. The Blue Economy proposes that "the waste of one product becomes the input to create a new cash flow" (Pauli 2010). This is very much the same as industrial ecology, but with more of a focus on the human labor side of things. Relatedly, the Biosphere Rules are a guide for implementing a closed-loop system of production and consumption (Unruh 2008). These perspectives add slight variations to the same themes.

> **Circular Economy:** A shift in economic development and regulatory frameworks that replaces linear take–make–waste systems of production and consumption with circular approaches. Closed-loop and cradle-to-cradle design processes are key attributes, but circular economy encompasses the larger socioeconomic context to enable the widespread use of these design strategies.

At the level of the organization, this means a transition of business models to those that prioritize producer responsibility and a shift in thinking from selling products to product–service systems and collaborative models of consumption (i.e., the sharing economy). It also opens space for new business models to emerge that we have yet to identify as more elaborate interactions between industries are created.

There has, however, been an interesting twist in the naming of the circular economy as a unique idea. Championed in recent years by the Ellen MacArthur Foundation, this new movement of bioinspired business was first named in a report by McKinsey & Company, one of the world's leading business consulting firms. They re-packaged the provocations of the early work in industrial ecological thinking into a business and economic acumen that has gained immense traction. Their January 2012 report, entitled *Towards the Circular Economy: Economic and Business Rationale for an Accelerated Transition* lays out some of the more practical aspects of making this transition, and by December that same year, the European Commission echoed the need for a circular economy in another report. By 2015, they had begun major projects in China, Brazil, and the United States. By early 2017, they had 12 major partners and nearly 100 members of their Circular Economy 100 innovation program. This is a tremendous amount of traction in a very short amount of time! For a manager, the Ellen MacArthur Foundation offers several business programs related to plastics and other resource flows. With the Circular Economy 100 and Project Mainstream initiatives, they intend to create a cross-sector, cross-industry pre-competitive space to discuss opportunities and challenges with circular economy models. They provide spaces to collaborate, educational programs, publications, and partnerships to help advance a company's or a government's circular economy agenda.

The circular economy space is a very exciting one at the moment. There is a great deal of energy and momentum, and more players are getting involved all the time. Not to mention that the business case is well-developed and new financing models are also emerging. For many businesses, engagement with the circular economy is an opportunity to stay ahead of more stringent waste management and recycling regulations that are likely on the horizon. While it is once again the repackaging of ideas come and gone, this new repackaging seems to have attracted the right people, with the right resources, at the right moment in history.

Conclusion

As you can tell, the jump from the organizational to the enterprise and economic context requires a broader level of consideration than usual. It begs questions of the larger socioeconomic and political factors that influence innovation for sustainability, and in many instances, it challenges the status quo of business strategy. Many users of biological inspiration value it for its ability to evoke expansive thinking and open up the potential solution space to alternatives previously not considered (Mead 2017; Tempelman, de Pauw, van der Grinten, Ernst-Jan, and Grevers 2015). And that, it surely does.

CHAPTER 7

Processes and Conceptual Tools

As you can imagine, there are now a number of different processes, approaches, and conceptual tools available across disciplines. While engineering, architecture, design, and other disciplines each have their own discipline-specific approaches, this chapter will provide resources for a more general audience that is new to bioinspired innovation. This is in no way an exhaustive list, particularly as many tools have emerged in different languages (e.g., German, French, Japanese), but it will give you a sampling of some of the more and less technical approaches to industrial ecology, cradle to cradle, biomimicry, and circular economy.

Tools for Industrial Ecology

Industrial ecology now has a legacy of nearly 30 years, and as such, many of the tools to support it are widely used and accepted. They frequently go by other names and have been rebranded and repackaged many times. Most of these tools come from engineering disciplines and include approaches to modeling and measuring supply chains. A few tools that you may encounter (in no particular order) include environmental management systems, environmental impact assessments, life cycle assessments, material flow analysis, and full cost accounting. It is likely that your organization, if it produces things and a sustainability report, uses some variation of these tools. Modeling tools such as stock and flow analysis and agent-based modeling are also used to create systems views of resource considerations. These are specialized approaches that usually require training with specific software applications, but the tools are common enough now that many specialists have acquired these skills.

Tools for Cradle to Cradle Design

The most recent cradle-to-cradle movement, as described by William McDonough and Michael Braungart (Braungart and McDonough 2009), is now supported by a number of tools, websites, certifications, and consultants.

Probably the most commonly known tool is a certification managed by the Cradle to Cradle Products Innovation Institute (www.c2ccertified.org). This certification is intended to be a consumer-facing indicator of a certain level of quality in the life cycle management of a product. The certification has gained traction in recent years, though it is still arguable whether it adds value in terms of marketability and consumer receptiveness.

The C2C-Centre also hosts a variety of tools on their website (www.c2c-centre.com/tools) that have been created by members of the cradle-to-cradle community. This includes guides for materials management onsite, how to inventory with cradle-to-cradle considerations, communication, and valuation tools for cradle-to-cradle products. It also includes a database called Continuous Loops where companies can add their waste streams and the resources they need to identify where exchanges can be made. As a business park manager, you can create a cluster in your area to enable resource exchange among participating businesses and manufacturers.

Tools for Biomimicry and Biomimetics

Kristina Wanieck and her colleagues in biomimetic research have curated a collection of 40 bioinspired tools and have identified a few patterns. Broadly speaking, the bioinspired design process has four basic steps: an idea to explore; accessing of the biology; a technological application; and the identification of a market niche. In addition to these four phases, they also identified three gaps that require specific skills sets to overcome, as shown in Figure 7.1. For our purposes, we will refer to these skill sets (developed by Tim McGee of LikoLabs) as:

Skills Required for Bioinspired Innovation
- Accessing biological knowledge
- Building language bridges
- Developing innovative solutions

Source: Tim McGee of LikoLabs.

Each of the tools included here supports the application of bioinspiration in various ways, some of them for specific skills and some of them for all three skills. For instance, BioTriz is a tool for accessing biological knowledge, and the Biomimicry Design Spiral is a process that addresses all three gaps with one approach. They each have their strengths and weaknesses that we will also discuss in this chapter.

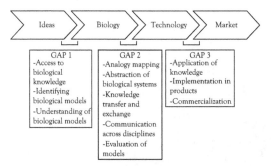

Figure 7.1 Gaps in the biomimetic design process and their underlying challenges

Source: Adapted from Wanieck, Fayemi, Maranzana, Zollfrank, and Jacobs (2017).

AskNature and the Biomimicry Design Toolbox

One of the most popular tools for general audiences and designers is a search engine of nature's functions called AskNature (www.AskNature.org). The concept is that you enter any function that you need to perform as a "what would nature do?" sort of question, such as "How does nature sense movement?" and what comes back are different organisms, ecosystems, and biomimetic innovations that sense movement. It is also a searchable repository of videos, activities, and lesson plans on bioinspiration.

The website is also organized conceptually according to function, with something called the Biomimicry Taxonomy (Figure 7.2). This is a useful tool for building bridge language between the biology and application. For instance, if a designer is looking to create a stronger plastic water bottle, they may start with the group of functions "Protect from physical harm" and then move down into the subgroup "Prevent structural failure" until you find a function that might help you think about your problem differently. Or you can just start at the *Functions* level and work your way around until something strikes you as a new way to solve your challenge.

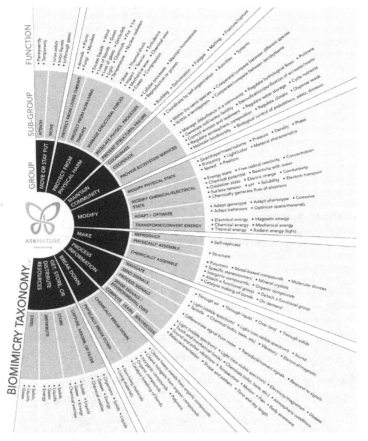

Figure 7.2 Biomimicry Taxonomy (AskNature.org)

This is a bit of an aside, but it is important to note that the functional perspective of AskNature.org is just one way to view biological strategies for problem solving. Other various laws and patterns have also been identified, named, and sometimes, modeled mathematically. Common visual patterns include symmetries, branching, spirals, meanders, waves, bubbles, and stripes. You may have heard of references to fractal patterns, the Fibonacci sequence, or Murray's law that determines the necessary diameters for optimized flow in a branches system. (Note that it is not Murphy's Law—the one about how things that can go wrong, will go wrong.) These patterns are commonly referred to in biomimetic innovation and are worth noting along with Life's Principles and other such biological and ecological phenomena and strategies.

This way of using bioinspiration is very much a creative process, and in the case of AskNature.org, the Biomimicry Institute, who created and manage the site, have created an entire suite of creative tools and methods to guide you through. The Biomimicry Toolbox (toolbox.biomimicry.org) contains a collection of core concepts and methods that are easily accessible for a general audience.

One such tool is the Biomimicry Design Spiral (Figure 7.3), created by Carl Hastrich (2005 https://biomimicry.org/biomimicry-design-spiral/). The Design Spiral has six phases that are intended to be visited iteratively to solve an existing design challenge. The first phase is to *Identify* your real challenge and the functions that you are trying to perform, for example, create a new way to access clean water in rural places. The next step is to

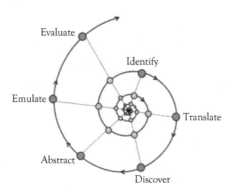

Figure 7.3 Biomimicry Design Spiral

Source: Graphic courtesy of Biomimicry Institute (www.biomimicry.org)

Translate that challenge into functional bridge language that can be used to access the biology, as is done with the Biomimicry Taxonomy. Then *Discover* natural models by going outside, asking a biologist, looking in biology books, or searching AskNature.org. From there, you *Abstract* out the design principles from the biology, creating a bridge language back from the biology to the design space again. AskNature.org does this for you already. The next step is to *Emulate* biology that inspires you into a design solution. And the final phase is to *Evaluate* the effectiveness of your design, both for solving the challenge and to address sustainability concerns. Once you get through this process once, it may be helpful to take another loop around the spiral to address some other aspect of the design as well. Or do this process in rapid succession to quickly vet possible solutions and narrow the solution space. It can be a helpful tool to align a design team using bioinspiration because it creates a common language for the process.

Biomimetics for Engineers

For the more engineering types, there are also numerous tools and approaches. We will just talk about a four here: Structure-Behavior-Function models, BioTriz, ISO standards, and software.

One of the most difficult tasks for non-biologists is to access biology at a level deeper than simply the observable characteristics such as color, size, and location. After teaching biology to engineering students for several classes at Georgia Tech, Ashok Goel and his colleagues developed a method for understanding complex natural systems by breaking them down into three categories of observation: Structure-Behavior-Function. This *ontology*, as they call it, evokes the innovator to see natural systems with three different perspectives to reduce the complexity of observation. The *Structure* refers to the "What?," or the stuff of the system. These are frequently the physical components. The *Behavior*, then, is the "How?" How does the system perform its necessary functions and respond to its environment. The *Function* refers to the "Why?" of the system, or the reason the system is structured and behaves as it does within its context. This is a simple method to break down complex natural systems into accessible components that can then be translated into innovative solutions (Helms, Vattam, Goel, and Yen 2011).

The next engineering-derived tool is called BioTRIZ. It is based on the TRIZ systematic problem-solving methodology that derived patterns from the inventions found in the global collection of patents. Through this process of pattern-seeking, they identified 40 Inventive Principles and 39 Engineering Parameters that can inform a design challenge. In the case of BioTRIZ, Julian Vincent and his colleagues at the University of Bath, United Kingdom, created a similar methodology, but rather than looking at the patents of the world, they are looking at the organisms of the world through a similar pattern-seeking lens. Similarly to the Structure-Behavior-Function approach, this method follows this mantra "Things (substance, structure) do things (requiring energy and information) somewhere (space, time)." By dividing problems and their potential solutions into this framework, it opens up the solution space and enables the translation of biological functions into that space (Helfman-Cohen and Reich 2017).

The International Standards Organization (ISO) has recently developed a set of standards related to biomimetics, ISO/TC 266. The existing standards are entitled: Biomimetic materials, structures and components; Terminology, concepts and methodology; and Biomimetic structural optimization. At the time of writing, there were also a few other standards in progress, though a timeline for release was not clear. One caveat to these standards: while ISO/TC 266 is intending to be an international authoritative guide to biomimetic practices, it still represents the views of a small subset of academics and practitioners from around the globe. These standards are in no way inclusive of all possible approaches and resources, and are rather a sampling of preferred practices. It is just something to keep in mind if you come from a culture that values protocols and standards. In choosing a standardized method, you do not choose any other number of possible methods.

One last note related to engineering approaches is the use of software. There are a number of discipline-specific software programs that have emerged over the years. Without going into much detail and to avoid the endorsement of any particular product, I will only say that a quick search for *biomimetic software* can open up many options to help you address specific engineering needs such as optimization, biomorphic translation, biomimetic simulations, and various measurements of biomimetic systems.

Tools for Circular Economy

The majority of tools and resources available to innovate with the circular economy can be found within the sphere of the Ellen MacArthur Foundation. The most practical of these tools was produced in collaboration with IDEO, a world-renowned product design and design thinking firm. Together, they produced a collection of tools and methods called the Circular Design Guide (www.circulardesignguide.com). The guide provides an easily shareable introduction to the subject for a general audience, a series of approaches to the design process, and some insights into the mindset shift necessary to start thinking in circular systems.

At the time of writing, there was also a process underway by the British Standards Institute (BSI) to develop a set of guidelines and best practices related to the circular economy. It was still early days in their process, but given the current trajectory of circular economy efforts, it is likely that this will result in meaningful recommendations for implementation.

Conclusion

As you can see, a wide array of bioinspired tools already exist across several disciplines to help you implement innovative solutions in a variety of contexts. There are numerous other tools that address discipline-specific needs and just as many professional consultants who are able to assist business managers with these tools. If you are interested in further resources, please refer to the resource list at the end of the book.

Next we will spend some time talking about some of the practical issues related to culture, habit, and the implementation of bioinspired innovation.

CHAPTER 8

Thinking Strategically

While teaching workshops with this material in corporate settings, I have witnessed some participants have strong gut reactions to the idea that everything is changing all of the time, and others who find it very difficult to accept that nature might have more elegant solutions than human ingenuity. And to be honest, I have not really been able to understand why some people cling to stability and institutions, while others seem to reject the notion that anything is ever stable and view change as the only constant. I am sure that there is a plethora of psychological research available on this subject, but for our purposes, I will only say that this is something to be aware of if you try to utilize any of these models in your organization. Expect resistance. You may even be able to anticipate the types of resistance that you will come across, depending on the culture of your organization. This chapter will give some insights into the various cultures of innovating organizations, some of the pitfalls to be aware of, and some potential alternative routes if you are having difficulty utilizing bioinspiration inside your organization.

Cultures of Sustainability-Oriented Innovation

A major focus of my research related to bioinspiration is to understand why some organizations seem to jump in with full commitment, while others toy around for a while and the momentum for bioinspiration eventually fizzles out. To investigate these issues, I have compared three sets of characteristics: (1) characteristics of bioinspiration as an innovation, (2) characteristics of the business unit attempting to use bioinspiration, and (3) characteristics of the innovation context, including the entire business and the overall socioeconomic context of the bioinspired innovation process. Through a large number of interviews, I learned that generally speaking, people using bioinspiration tended to view it in similar ways across organizations, regardless of their outcomes. They view it as complex, but no more complex than other innovation processes, and they value it for its ability to expand the potential solution space into a set of ideas they never would have conceived otherwise. The characteristics of the business unit were highly variable, with a few patterns emerging, but in general, they did not make or break success with bioinspired innovation processes. However, the factors that were most influential were related to the innovation context. A few strong patterns emerged that go a long way to explain why some organizations succeed with these tools and some do not. I call them sustainability-oriented innovation narratives, and I hope that one of them illuminates your organizational situation and needs.

Broadly speaking, it is a combination of sustainability cultures, innovation cultures and infrastructure, and leadership engagement that influence the results of bioinspired innovation processes. The combination of these factors creates one of the three sustainability-oriented innovation cultures: *Ambiguous*, *Accountable*, and *Aspirational*.

Ambiguous Organizations

Ambiguous organizations typically have a hard time describing what sustainability means for them, and there are several inconsistent narratives described by different people across the organization. There is little sense of sustainability leadership, and most of their sustainability initiatives are motivated by efficiency and cost savings. They tend to use bioinspiration outside of their traditional innovation channels and see it as a radical approach. The individuals who bring bioinspiration into these organizations frequently depart for any number of reasons, but express frustration with internal politics, lack of support for innovation efforts, or elitist leadership cultures.

Accountable Organizations

Accountable organizations, on the other hand, have very strong sustainability cultures that are deeply embedded in the corporate identity and management structures. They tend to focus on ethically motivated initiatives that consider the triple-bottom line accounting and tracking. The existing sustainability narratives are so strong, in fact, that they find it hard to reinvent them when presented with the opportunity to do so. When innovation and sustainability management present the senior leadership with nature as the model for sustainability, the idea has difficulty gaining traction because the current sustainability narratives and accounting systems are so entrenched throughout the organization. And when they are faced with difficult financial times, sustainability and innovation are reduced to meet the expectations of shareholders. They typically have sustainability departments with sophisticated tools to track and improve sustainability metrics. These metrics guide much of their innovation process and are a required aspect for new product development processes. They try many different bioinspired tools and approaches in ideation sessions and are well-versed in how each of the tools compare and contrast. However, despite all of this effort to achieve radical sustainability-oriented innovations, they usually only manage to accomplish incremental innovations within prescribed innovation timelines and processes. They have some success with bioinspiration, but generally describe it as just another tool in their toolbox and find it mildly disappointing. The management that has tried to push radical innovation for sustainability may get frustrated and leave the organization.

Aspirational Organizations

In aspirational organizations, their sustainability agenda is intrinsically motivated, aimed at restorative practices, and nature is *the* standard for sustainability throughout the organizational ranks. These organizations also have a long history of sustainability in their culture, though people describe several different phases of this history, with periods of reinvention in their cultural narrative. They view themselves as role models and leaders for sustainability-oriented innovation, and while they do measure progress, their organizations and innovation processes are led by an intrinsically motivated sustainability narrative, rather than incremental efficiencies. While they feel pressures to make trade-offs between long-term success with innovation and sustainability and short-term cost-efficiency needs, they do not compromise on their values amidst financial pressures. They do not try to manage innovation with hierarchies or any particular tools and processes, and they do not describe the various bioinspired tools with much distinction. They rather rely on a "freedom to fail" as their guiding innovation mantra. Rather than trying to create bioinspired products, they are trying to be like nature in their operations, and if that results in a product innovation, it is a particularly big win.

Table 8.1 compares and contrasts these three sustainability-oriented innovation narratives. While they are full of nuance and subtlety,

Table 8.1 Sustainability oriented innovation narratives influencing bioinspiration

	Ambiguous	Accountable	Aspirational
Sustainability is...	...political and economically motivated.	...practice and ethically motivated.	...purpose and intrinsically motivated.
Sustainability activities...	...are mentioned in annual reports. "Sustainability is hard to implement because it's such a broad word."	...must be measured for everything. "As a large international company, we feel responsible for what we do."	... must be modeled for others. "We use our business activities to become restorative through the power of our influence."
Our sustainability culture is...	...very weak.	...very strong.	...to compare ourselves to nature.
Innovation is...	...usually incremental and not usually driven by sustainability.	...an important part of our culture and is highly managed.	...something that happens, but we do not try to manage it.
Bioinspiration is approached...	...as an experimental approach to innovation.	...as one of the several approaches to innovation for sustainability in our usual R&D processes.	...as a mindset that guides our company-wide approach to sustainability and innovation.
Our leadership...	...is not really involved in bioinspired innovation processes.	...is fully supportive of our sustainability efforts, but view bioinspiration as a project in the R&D department.	...is intimately familiar with bioinspiration and views it as an important part of the company's agenda.

Source: Adapted from Mead (2017).

hopefully, some aspect resonates with your situation. It is helpful to know where your starting point is so as to better identify potential hurdles and roadblocks along the way. We will talk about some of those roadblocks next.

Trials and Tribulations of Managing Innovation Inspired by Nature

While there has been a great deal of excitement around the biomimetic promise, there has also been a lot of hype. It is important to recognize that people may feel a bit jaded or skeptical about such grand expectations. Here are some things to look out for as someone trying to implement bioinspired innovation.

First, it ultimately needs to be a better solution—not simply a bioinspired solution—to survive in the marketplace. The best of bioinspired intentions with beautiful stories and images may be an entry point for some customers, but it does not necessarily mean it is worth a premium in the marketplace. Similarly, bioinspired certifications do not necessarily draw that premium from consumers—some do, but this is far from guaranteed. For this reason, it is particularly important to use these tools in an expansive way, to promote radical innovation, rather than incremental changes to existing products. The R&D investment has to be worth it, and this can be difficult in existing products.

Relatedly, leadership must also be supportive of radical innovation efforts, and it is helpful if they can see the value of bioinspiration beyond the realm of the project. This is a way of viewing problem solving, not simply innovation outcomes. Many companies aim for the *easy win* and find themselves disappointed and discouraged when it is not so easy. This is happening for a lot of reasons, but a big part of the problem is that there are no easy wins. Bioinspired innovation is probably 60 percent mindset shift to view nature as a model and 40 percent the actual work of innovating. This must be understood as part of the overall process. This makes the bean counters very nervous because they hate waiting to count their beans, but it is important that leadership understands this distinction.

Beware of fatigue of sustainability-oriented innovation. Several companies that I spoke with talked about trying many different innovation tools and approaches; so many that they were rather bored of ideation sessions. These people had all the tools, and they were not particularly impressed by any of them. The creative process had gotten to be dull. Clearly, this creates problems for innovation if people are tired of being innovative. The main recommendation that I have to avoid this scenario is to give people training and space to be innovative—and then expect nothing in return. In some of the most innovative cultures in the world, innovation is everyone's job. It is not a department, an assignment, a project, or a job title. It is a way of thinking about the world and about the work. The maintenance of innovative thinking is the priority, rather than innovation outcomes.

One final note is related to the management of bioinspired innovation processes and teams. Many individuals who lead the way on these types of projects, the champion of the effort, are also likely some of the most forward thinking and visionary employees. They are the early adopters of many sustainability practices and are always scanning the horizon for what is new and exciting. If they have gone through an immersive, intensive training in biomimicry or some other approach, they may have experienced a personal transformation and view their relationship to natural systems and sustainability much more intensely than they did before—and they will want to implement changes with this newfound knowledge. Several of my interviewees, particularly in those organizations with Ambiguous and Accountable narratives related to sustainability-oriented innovation, had this experience, and when they came up against too many barriers to implement changes, they moved on to greener pastures elsewhere, taking their knowledge and institutional memory with them. They move on to teach, start consultancies, and join other sectors to try again to utilize their sustainability passions. After hearing enough of these stories, I started to think that perhaps there is some larger phenomenon happening. I began to refer to it as *Sustainability Brain Drain*. This specific type of brain drain may result in a net loss of sustainability momentum across multinationals because thought leadership migrates to other sectors. As a manager, if you are investing a lot of money and time training your employees in sustainability, it is probably worthwhile to nurture that investment in other ways to ensure that your organization benefits from it.

Managing the Challenges of Implementation

There are some challenges that are consistent across all cultures and some that are specific to certain cultures. We will start by looking at pointers for managing bioinspiration in all organizational types and then talk about hurdles specific to different cultures.

In general, designers are important in bioinspired processes and should be considered an important part of the team. Of all of the disciplinary specializations—ranging from engineering to biology to management—it is the inclusion of designers in the bioinspired innovation process that seems to be the most consequential for project results. My gut tells me that this is because of a few main skills that designers possess. First, they are trained to be systems thinkers from a transdisciplinary perspective. They are transdisciplinary in the sense that they view the problem space from a multitude of perspectives simultaneously and combine data points from a bird's eye view. Their training is a combination of technical expertise and social observation, which allows them to translate biological function to a wide variety of contexts. They are uniquely equipped to take full advantage of the cognitive benefits that biological inspiration can offer such as expansive thinking, imaginative applications, and alternative future scenarios. And finally, they may have a unique perspective that enables them to bridge with external consultants, suppliers, and R&D organizations for partnerships that enable success with bioinspiration, which leads us to our next troubleshooting strategy: outsourcing.

Many internal innovation and design units are well-versed in the new product development process. Some are so effective, in fact, that they cannot see any other way to do it besides the ways that they have always been effective. For those Ambiguous and Accountable organizations, the complete outsourcing of bioinspired innovation may be an effective strategy to overcome organizational barriers. Many organizations work closely with consultants who specialize in bioinspiration, but attempt to do much of the innovation work internally. And many of them end up frustrated because they cannot get much done within their organizations, no matter how much training and consultation they expose themselves to along the way. For these organizations, it might be more effective to hire a firm or university research lab that can do all of the new product development for them within the negotiated terms of an intellectual property arrangement. It is difficult to know when to choose this route, but if you know that this has been an issue in the past, you may want to rethink your overall vision for how innovation gets done within your organization.

As mentioned briefly, many organizations get caught up with identifying the low-hanging fruit or easy wins using biologically inspired innovation strategies. They may look at existing needs assessments, consumer research, or existing innovation challenges that they have already identified and charge ahead with a solutions-driven process. However, after 10 years in this field with over 30 clients and over 100 interviews and surveys with bioinspired innovators, I have come to believe that it is not the most effective approach. These days, I am of the view that we need to train professionals in bioinspired innovation strategies to create culture, not to create products. Tools, skills, and mindsets are all important components of the development of this culture, but they should be framed as a toolset to create a culture of bioinspired design, rather than a toolset to create bioinspired products. This subtle shift does several things to the innovation process. First, it puts the emphasis on learning and giving people the space to explore new ideas to see what emerges. Second, it removes some of the performance pressure that comes with product-focused outcomes. I can think of nothing more stifling to the innovation process than overwhelming front-end considerations of return on investment. Finally, it allows users to co-develop criteria for success within their unique circumstances. Of course, seeking a certification requires a completely different approach, but if the goal is to seek inspiration from natural systems, this can mean many, many things.

The next pointer applies specifically to Accountable organizations, but may also be applicable in other contexts. Accountable organizations are deeply committed to sustainability, and they are also very effective at tracking the progress of this commitment. So much so, that they may get bogged down with sustainability criteria, checklists, and accounting processes. For innovators accustomed to working in this space, bioinspiration can feel like yet another layer of management in the innovation process and be stifling to the creative process. One way to avoid this may be to incorporate bioinspired strategies into existing design checklists. For instance, design guidelines such as using water-based chemistry, closed-loop manufacturing, or the use of locally available materials can easily be modified to integrate with existing design criteria related to toxicity, material selection, and sourcing requirements. This integration embeds biological insights into existing processes without creating an additional layer that may be burdensome to the innovation process.

Tips for Implementing Bioinspired Innovation
- Use bioinspiration as an expansive innovation approach, rather than a rigid, linear process
- Leadership needs to be supportive of the inherent ambiguity often present during radial innovation processes
- Beware of innovation fatigue
- Do not let sustainability accounting drive your innovation processes. If this seems impossible to avoid, outsource it
- Remember that low-hanging fruit and radical innovations are incompatible approaches
- Include design expertise on your team
- Connect with nature whenever you can and inspire your team to do the same.
- Prevent sustainability brain drain by giving employees an outlet for their newly acquired interests, skills, and passions.

The last point to mention about overcoming challenges is specifically related to the avoidance of sustainability brain drain. Creative visionary types need an outlet for transformative experiences and perspectives. Actually, we all do. As mentioned earlier, there is a growing body of research related to the biophilia hypothesis suggesting that we seek connections with nature because we are hard-wired to do so. Denying these connections can have serious consequences for our physical and mental health. As a manager, you may be in a unique position to support these innate biophilic tendencies in a way that can improve the overall performance of your organization. I have heard of a few ways that managers are doing this. For instance, Yvon Chouinard, founder of Patagonia (an outdoor apparel company with a strong sustainability ethic), wrote a book entitled *Let My People Go Surfing* (Chouinard 2006) in which he describes how it is part of the company culture to set their jobs to the side for a moment and go surfing when the surfing is good. He actively encourages his employees to respect, enjoy, and act as stewards for and in natural places in all aspects of their life, not just during their free time. It is an embedded part of their culture. I have heard of a few other managers supporting their employees in *walk and talk* meetings outdoors and the creation of nature-nerd groups as ways to enable nature-inspired innovation. The possibilities are really endless if the will to engage with Life this way is strong enough.

Conclusion

This chapter has addressed some of the practicalities of bioinspired innovation in a candid way. Derived from research to avoid too much anecdotal input, this chapter gets at some of the major challenges and how one might avoid repeating the same mistakes as those before them. Every innovation culture is unique, but a few patterns do emerge when it comes to this process. It is hoped that this chapter represents the beginning of an ongoing conversation to further our collective knowledge and capabilities in this area.

CHAPTER 9

Conclusion

The goal of this book has been to equip you, a busy management professional, with the basics of learning from nature, both conceptually and practically. You will recall that we began with an analysis of the three conceptions of how business, society, and nature are related. For bioinspiration to be effective as an approach to innovation for sustainability, we must begin to more readily view our organizations as embedded in social and ecological systems, rather than the separateness that we currently accept in our economic growth models. We also must carefully consider whether we are aiming to be sustainable, resilient, or regenerative with our innovation goals and not conflate these concepts, but rather connect with the larger bodies of theory.

We have covered a range of tools, approaches, and certifications to be applied at various scales. Bioinspiration can be applied as metaphor or analogy in management, operations, product development, and for enterprise-level changes. And the approaches presented here only scratch the surface of what is possible. The more familiar and comfortable users become with the process of learning from nature, the more expansive the innovation space becomes. Over the years, my bioinspired colleagues and I have discussed how it has trickled into every aspect of our lives, our relationships, and even our approach to child rearing. Once you drink the proverbial Kool-Aid, it can be hard to shake this way of thinking.

This book has also addressed some very practical and tactical issues associated with bioinspiration, including different cultures of adopting organizations and how to manage difficulties in the implementation process. Organizations have unique cultures, expectations, and needs for many things, and bioinspiration is no exception. Outside experts can go a long way to help you along the process, but no one knows an organization better than those on the inside. It is important that you incorporate this institutional knowledge into a bioinspired innovation process as much as possible. If your consultant team does not seem to understand this, demand better. Or perhaps, it is best to frame your innovation process in terms of cultural development, rather than product development. On the other hand, it may just be more appropriate to outsource it altogether. Talk to as many consultants as possible before you choose one that matches your culture and needs. This is not a one-size-fits-all endeavor and requires a customized approach that matches your expectations.

Innovation is a science and an art simultaneously. It is a science, in that one must observe and clearly understand the facts of the situation, recognize the most important data points to enable change, and identify the malleable components of the system. It is an art, in that it involves imagining a new future outcome that does not yet exist, identifying the social, economic, and ecological resources that are possible, necessary, and available, and putting the components in place to realize that future potential. Bioinspired innovation epitomizes this intersection of science and art. And hopefully, this book has helped you to see some clear pathways to create this intersection for yourself.

Further Reading

In addition to the cited references following this section, this resource list is intended as a glimpse into the vast world of bioinspired innovation. The bioinspiration community has done a great job of compiling resource lists. Two collections that I highly recommend are:

Think Biomimicry (www.thinkingbiomimicry.com) curated by Rachel Hahs, a biomimicry facilitator in the Chicago area. This is the most extensive collection of biomimicry resources out there. Start here and if you still do not find something that suits your interests, keep reading this list.

Biomimicry Professional Book List (Search for BProfessional book list on Pinterest), curated by Joe Zazzera. This is the most complete bioinspired book collection that I have seen as well.

A Few Other Bioinspired Basics

- AskNature.org—A search engine of nature's strategies and functions.
- Biomimicry Institute—www.biomimicry.org—The world's most recognized source for biomimicry resources and community. You can also find a network near you on their website.
- Symbiosis Group—Symbiosisgroup.com—My consultancy website offers further resources.
- Biomimicry 3.8—www.biomimicry.net—Janine Benyus and Dayna Baumeister's consultancy with an impressive client history.
- European Biomimicry Alliance—www.biomimicryalliance.eu/ —A central hub for Europe's growing biomimicry community.

- Ellen MacArthur Foundation—www.ellenmacarthur-foundation.org/—The most prominent organization in the circular economy.
- KARIM Network (2015)—www.karimnetwork.com/wp-content/uploads/2015/02/Guide_Biomimicry_online.pdf—Introduction to Nature Inspired Solutions: A guide for entrepreneurs and innovation support organizations to implement biomimicry as a tool for responsible innovation.
- Donella H. Meadows (1997)—Places to Intervene in a System.
- Hoagland and Dodson (1995)—The Way Nature Works.

References

Adams, R., S. Jeanrenaud, J. Bessant, D. Denyer, and P. Overy. 2016. "Sustainability-Oriented Innovation: A Systematic Review." *International Journal of Management Reviews* 18, no. 2, pp. 180–205. http://doi.org/http://doi.org/10.1111/ijmr.12068

Benyus, J. 1997. *Biomimicry: Innovation Inspired by Nature.* HarperCollins.

Biomimicry 3.8. n.d. Life's Principles. www.biomimicry.net. Retrieved 30 September 30, 2017.

Bonabeau, E., and C. Meyer. 2001. "Swarm Intelligence : A Whole New Way to Think About Business." *Harvard Business Review*, May, pp. 106–14.

Bonser, R.H.C. 2006. "Patented Biologically-Inspired Technological Innovations: A Twenty Year View." *Journal of Bionic Engineering* 3, no. 1, pp. 39–41. http://doi.org/10.1016/S1672-6529(06)60005-X

Borland, H., and A. Lindgreen. 2012. "Sustainability, Epistemology, Ecocentric Business, and Marketing Strategy: Ideology, Reality, and Vision." *Journal of Business Ethics* 117, no. 1, pp. 173–87. http://doi.org/10.1007/s10551-012-1519-8

Braungart, M., and W. McDonough. 2009. *Cradle to Cradle: Remaking the Way We Make Things.* Random House.

Capra, F., and P.L. Luisi. 2014. *The Systems View of Life: A Unifying Vision.* Cambridge University Press.

Chouinard, Y. 2006. *Patagonia: Let My People Go Surfing: The Education of a Reluctant Businessman.* Penguin Books.

Dobson, A. 1998. *Justice and the Environment: Conceptions of Environmental Sustainability.* Oxford University Press.

Du Plessis, C., and P. Brandon. 2014. "An Ecological Worldview as Basis for a Regenerative Sustainability Paradigm for the Built Environment." *Journal of Cleaner Production* 109, pp. 53–61. http://doi.org/10.1016/j.jclepro.2014.09.098

Dubberly, H. 2008. "Design in the Age of Biology." *ACM Interactions.* Oct. v.XV.5

Ehrenfeld, J. 2003. "Putting a Spotlight on Metaphors and Analogies in Industrial Ecology." *Journal of Industrial Ecology* 7, no. 1, pp. 1–4. http://doi.org/10.1162/108819803766729131

Ehrenfeld, J.R. 2008. *Sustainability by Design: A Subversive Strategy for Transforming Our Consumer Culture.* Yale University Press.

Elkington, J. 1997. *Cannibals With Forks: The Triple Bottom Line of 21st Century Business.* Oxford: Capstone Publishing Ltd.

Floyd, M., and S. Gladwin. 2015. "Towards Sustainable 'Biofriendly' Materials for Additive Manufacturing." Spark.

Frosch, R.A., and N.E. Gallopoulos. 1989. "Strategies for Manufacturing." *Scientific American* 189, no. 3, pp. 144–52.

Gaziulusoy, A.I. 2015. "A Critical Review of Approaches Available for Design and Innovation Teams Through the Perspective of Sustainability Science and System Innovation Theories." *Journal of Cleaner Production* 107, (January), pp. 366–77. http://doi.org/10.1016/j.jclepro.2015.01.012

Ginsberg, A.D., J. Calvert, P. Schyfter, A. Eflick, and D. Endy. 2014. *Synthetic Aesthetics: Investigating Synthetic Biology's Designs on Nature.* Cambridge, MA: London, UK: MIT Press.

Gleich, A., C. von, Pade, U. Petschow, and E. Pissarskoi. 2010. *Potentials and Trends in Biomimetics.* Berlin, Heidelberg: Springer Berlin Heidelberg. http://doi.org/10.1007/978-3-642-05246-0

Harman, J. 2013. *The Shark's Paintbrush: Biomimicry and How Nature is Inspiring Innovation.* London, UK: Nicholas Brealey Publishing.

Helfman Cohen, Y., and Y. Reich. 2017. *Biomimetic Design Method for Innovation and Sustainability.* Cham: Springer International Publishing. http://doi.org/10.1007/978-3-319-33997-9

Helms, M., S. Vattam, A.K. Goel, and J. Yen. 2011. "Enhanced Human Learning Using Structure-Behavior-Function Models." In *ICALT, IEEE 11th International Conference on Advanced Learning Technologies,* 239–43. Athens, GA.

Hock, D., and P.M. Senge. 2009. *One from Many: Visa and the Rise of Chaordic Organization.* ReadHowYouWant.com.

Hutchins, G. 2012. *The Nature of Business: Redesigning for Resilience.* Green Books.

Iansiti, M., and R. Levien. 2004. *The Keystone Advantage: What the New Dynamics of Business Ecosystems Mean for Strategy, Innovation, and Sustainability.* Harvard Business Press.

Institute, T.L.F. 2017. "The Living Future Institute." Retrieved August 4, 2017, from https://living-future.org/lbc/basics/

Johnson, E.R. 2011. *Reanimating Bios: Biomimetic Science and Empire.* University of Minnesota.

Kaye, H.L. 1997. *The Social Meaning of Modern Biology.* New Brunswick, New Jersey: Transaction Publishers.

Lin, Q., D. Gourdon, C.J. Sun, N. Holten-Andersen, T.H. Anderson, J.H. Waite, and J.N. Israelachvili. 2007. "Adhesion Mechanisms of the Mussel Foot Proteins mfp-1 and mfp-3." *Proceedings of the National Academy of Sciences of the United States of America* 104, no. 10, pp. 3782–86. http://doi.org/10.1073/pnas.0607852104

Marcus, J., E.C. Kurucz, and B.A. Colbert. 2010. "Conceptions of the Business-Society-Nature interface: Implications for Management Scholarship." *Business & Society* 49, no. 3, pp. 402–38. http://doi.org/10.1177/0007650310368827

McKeag, T. 2015. "Berkeley Center for Green Chemistry. (2015). How Nature Makes Things: Relevant Bio-Inspired Approaches." Spark.

Mead, T.L. 2017. *Factors Influencing the Adoption of Nature Inspired Innovation In Multinational Corporations.* PhD Thesis. Available online.

Mead, T.L., and S. Jeanrenaud. 2017. "The Elephant in the Room: Biomimetics and Sustainability." *Bioinspired, Biomimetic and Nanobiomaterials* 6, no. 2, pp. 113–21.

Okey, T.A. 2004. "Strategy as Ecology: Critique of the Keystone Advantage." *Harvard Business Review,* September, p. 132.

Pauli, G.A. 2010. *The Blue Economy: 10 Years, 100 Innovations, 100 Million Jobs.* Paradigm Publications.

Rifkin, J. 1999. *The Biotech Century: Harnessing the Gene and Remaking the World.* New York: Jeremy P. Tarcher/Putmam.

Romei, F. 2008. *Leonardo Da Vinci.* The Oliver Press, Inc.

Seebode, D., S. Jeanrenaud, and J. Bessant. 2012. "Managing Innovation for Sustainability." *R&D Management,* 42, no. 3, pp. 1–16.

Simonsen, S.H., R. Biggs, (Oonsie), M. Schlüter, M. Schoon, E. Bohensky, G. Cundill, V. Dakos, T. Daw, K. Kotschy, A. Leitch, and F. Moberg. 2014. "Applying Resilience Thinking: Seven Principles for Building Resilience in Social-Ecological Systems." *Stockolm Resilience Centre,* pp. 1–20.

Tempelman, E., I.C. de Pauw, B. van der Grinten, M. Ernst-Jan, and K. Grevers. 2015. "Biomimicry and Cradle-To-Cradle in Product Design: An Analysis of Current Design Practice." *Journal of Design Research* 13, no. 4, pp. 326–44.

The Fermanian Business and Economic Institute. 2010. *Global Biomimicry Efforts: An Economic Game Changer.*

Thompson, K., and R. Good. 2005. *Bioteaming Manifesto.* Available online.

Unruh, G.C. 2008. "The Biosphere Rules." *Harvard Business Review* 86, no. 2, February, pp. 111–17.

Wanieck, K., P.E. Fayemi, N. Maranzana, C. Zollfrank, and S. Jacobs. 2017. "Biomimetics and its Tools." *Bioinspired, Biomimetic and Nanobiomaterials* 6, no. 2, pp. 1–14. http://doi.org/10.1680/jbibn.16.00010

Woolley-Barker, T. 2017. *Teeming : How Superorganisms Work to Build : Infinite Wealth in a Finite World, (And Your Company Can Too).* White Cloud Press. Ashland, OR.

World Commission on Environment and Development. 1987. *Report of the World Commission on Environment and Development: Our Common Future.*

About the Author

Taryn Mead is an innovation and management scholar whose research focuses on the interface between corporate sustainability strategies and conceptualizations of nature. This includes subjects such as sustainability-oriented innovation, biomimicry, circular economy, the integration of planetary boundaries into corporate strategy, and the role of corporations in sustainable development. She also has experience in sustainable design and expertise in creativity for sustainability among design and engineering professionals in interdisciplinary settings. With early training as a biologist and post-graduate studies in the social sciences, she has developed an interest in the epistemological underpinnings of transdisciplinary topics and how this influences sustainability narratives across disciplines.

Before pursuing her PhD, Taryn worked as biologist, sustainability strategist, and Certified Biomimicry Professional consulting with over 30 corporate, municipal, and non-profit clients using biomimicry as a tool for innovation and sustainability. As a practitioner of nature-inspired innovation, she has worked on domestic and international projects ranging from new product design to industrial ecosystems to new cities for two million inhabitants. She has also served as the lead facilitator for numerous workshops with corporate clients and blossoming biomimics and lectured for large audiences.

Index

This book is a publication in support of the United Nations Principles for Responsible Management Education (PRME), housed in the UN Global Compact Office. The mission of the PRME initiative is to inspire and champion responsible management education, research and thought leadership globally. Please visit www.unprme.org for more information.

The Principles for Responsible Management Education Book Collection is edited through the Center for Responsible Management Education (CRME), a global facilitator for responsible management education and for the individuals and organizations educating responsible managers. Please visit www.responsiblemanagement.net for more information.

—Oliver Laasch, University of Manchester, Collection Editor

- *Teaching Ethics Across the Management Curriculum: Principles and Applications, Volume II* by Kemi Ogunyemi
- *Dark Sides of Business and Higher Education Management, Volume I* by Agata Stachowicz-Stanusch and Gianluigi Mangia
- *Dark Sides of Business and Higher Education Management, Volume II* by Agata Stachowicz-Stanusch and Gianluigi Mangia
- *Teaching Ethics Across the Management Curriculum: Contributing to a Global Paradigm Shift, Volume III* by Kemi Ogunyemi
- *Managing for Responsibility: A Sourcebook for an Alternative Paradigm* by Radha R. Sharma, Merrill Csuri, and Kemi Ogunyemi
- *Educating Social Entrepreneurs: From Idea Generation to Business Plan Formulation, Volume I* by Paul Miesing and Maria Aggestam
- *Educating Social Entrepreneurs: From Business Plan Formulation to Implementation, Volume II* by Paul Miesing and Maria Aggestam
- *Responsible Management Education: Some Voices From Asia* by Ranjini Swamy

Announcing the Business Expert Press Digital Library

Concise e-books business students need for classroom and research

This book can also be purchased in an e-book collection by your library as

- a one-time purchase,
- that is owned forever,
- allows for simultaneous readers,
- has no restrictions on printing, and
- can be downloaded as PDFs from within the library community.

Our digital library collections are a great solution to beat the rising cost of textbooks. E-books can be loaded into their course management systems or onto students' e-book readers. The **Business Expert Press** digital libraries are very affordable, with no obligation to buy in future years. For more information, please visit **www.businessexpertpress.com/librarians**. To set up a trial in the United States, please email **sales@businessexpertpress.com**.